The New Age Qabala Can Help You

In every person, the qualities essential for accelerating his or her growth and spiritual evolution are innate, but even those who recognize such potentials need an effective means of releasing them. The ancient and mystical Qabala *is that means!* Unfortunately, most of the literature and teachings on the Qabala is either too esoteric for those just starting their paths or the literature presumes a basic knowledge of the system and its operation most beginners would not have.

A person does not need to become a dedicated Qabalist in order to acquire benefits from its system. This book offers a simple understanding of what the Qabala is and how it operates. It provides practical methods and techniques so that the energies and forces within the system and within ourselves can be experienced in a manner that enhances growth and releases our greater potential. A student knowing *absolutely nothing* about the Qabala could read this and apply the methods with noticeable success.

Above the portals of the ancient Mystery Schools was but one commandment: "Know Thyself." Within each of us are *all* the energies and forces of the universe. Within each of us is the capability of releasing that infinite potential to manifest greater fulfillment, love and light into all arenas of our life. The Qabala provides us with the best means of recognizing and utilizing that potential, taking responsibility for our life and all the energies enacting within it.

The Qabala teaches us that there is *no one* doing anything that we also cannot do—in our own unique way. It shows us how to use what we learn in the best manner.

The Qabala shows us that the world is a world of *color, light and magic* that we can fashion to our highest dreams and ideals. It shows us that it is not complicated or relegated to some "gifted" few. The world of joy and magic is for *all*. It is a world that all may enter—but enter with openness and reverence—for this is also God's world.

About the Author

Ted Andrews is a full-time author, student and teacher in the metaphysical and spiritual fields. He conducts seminars, symposiums, and workshops and lectures throughout the country on many facets of ancient mysticism. Ted works with past-life analysis, auric interpretation, numerology, the Tarot and the Qabala as methods of developing and enhancing inner potential. He is a clairvoyant and certified in spiritual mediumship, basic hypnosis, and acupressure. Ted is also involved in the study and use of herbs as an alternative path. In addition to writing several books, he is a contributing author to various metaphysical magazines.

To Write to the Author

If you wish to contact the author or would like more information about this book, please write to the author in care of Llewellyn Worldwide, and we will forward your request. Both the author and publisher appreciate hearing from you and learning of your enjoyment of this book and how it has helped you. Llewellyn Worldwide cannot guarantee that every letter written to the author can be answered, but all will be forwarded. Please write to:

Ted Andrews
c/o Llewellyn Worldwide
P.O. Box 64383-015, St. Paul, MN 55164-0383, U.S.A.
Please enclose a self-addressed, stamped envelope for reply,
or $1.00 to cover costs.
If outside the U.S.A., enclose international postal reply coupon.

Free Catalog from Llewellyn

For more than 90 years Llewellyn has brought its readers knowledge in the fields of metaphysics and human potential. Learn about the newest books in spiritual guidance, natural healing, astrology, occult philosophy and more. Enjoy book reviews, new age articles, a calendar of events, plus current advertised products and services. To get your free copy of *Llewellyn's New Worlds of Mind and Spirit*, send your name and address to:

Llewellyn's New Worlds of Mind and Spirit
P.O. Box 64383-015, St. Paul, MN 55164-0383, U.S.A.

ABOUT LLEWELLYN'S NEW AGE SERIES

The "New Age"—it's a phrase we use, but what does it mean? Does it mean that we are entering the Aquarian Age? Does it mean that a new Messiah is coming to correct all that is wrong and make Earth into a Garden? Probably not—but the idea of a *major change* is there, combined with awareness that Earth *can* be a Garden; that war, crime, poverty, disease, etc., are not necessary "evils."

Optimists, dreamers, scientists . . . nearly all of us believe in a "better tomorrow," and that somehow we can do things now that will make for a better future life for ourselves and for coming generations.

In one sense, we all know there's nothing new under the Heavens, and in another sense that every day makes a new world. The difference is in our consciousness. And this is what the New Age is all about: it's a major change in consciousness found within each of us as we learn to bring forth and manifest powers that humanity has always potentially had.

Evolution moves in "leaps." Individuals struggle to develop talents and powers, and their efforts build a "power bank" in the Collective Unconsciousness, the soul of humanity that suddenly makes these same talents and powers easier access for the majority.

You still have to learn the "rules" for developing and applying these powers, but it is more like a "re-learning" than a *new* learning, because with the New Age it is as if the basis for these had become genetic.

Other Books by Ted Andrews

Animal-Speak
Dream Alchemy
Enchantment of the Faerie Realm
The Healer's Manual
How to Develop and Use Psychometry
How to Heal with Color
How to Meet & Work with Spirit Guides
How to See & Read the Aura
How to Uncover Your Past Lives
Imagick
Magickal Dance
The Magical Name
The Occult Christ
The Sacred Power in Your Name
Sacred Sounds

Llewellyn's New Age Series

Simplified Magic

A Beginner's Guide to the New Age Qabala

Ted Andrews

1995
Llewellyn Publications
St. Paul, Minnesota 55164-0383, U.S.A.

FIRST EDITION
Fifth Printing, 1995

CoverArt: Lissane Lake
Cover Design: Brooke Luteyn

Library of Congress Cataloging-in-Publication Data
Andrews, Ted, 1952-
    Simplified magic.

    (Llewellyn's new age series)
    Bibliography: p.
    1. Cabala. 2. Magic. I. Title.
BF1623.CA53   1988   135'.4   88-45192
ISBN 0-87542-015-X

Llewellyn Publications
A Division of Llewellyn Worldwide, Ltd.
P.O. Box 64383, St. Paul, MN 55164-0383

Dedication

To Kathy—whose faith, love and support
adds magic and wonder to my life.

Contents

archangels and angels that will assist us in awakening our own innate powers and abilities at each level of consciousness. The qualities that we can awaken and begin to utilize within our daily lives by touching each level.

ing of the Qabala. How paths and sephiroth within the Qabala adapt themselves to each individual.

The Qabala as a method of creating greater and more fulfilling realities. The Qabala as a means of re-creating our past, as well as our future. The importance of perseverence and practice. Balance and imbalance within the Qabala. Precautions and reminders for those starting their path of evolution.

Introduction

This is a book of magic. It contains no charms, no spells and no incantations. It is not a book of sleight of hand nor prestidigitation. Neither is it a manual for talismans and conjurings. And yet with all that it is not, it is still a book of magic. It is a book of Light.

It is not important whether or not you believe in magic. It is not important whether you believe in a Divine Light operating positively and actively throughout our universe. What is important in this world, as in all worlds, is that we each have the opportunity to expand our consciousness and our awareness—and in the process learn something new. What is important is being able to open our minds to the potential that resides within each of us, a potential that can be utilized individually to impact upon our environment with an effect that is both positive and enlightening. What is important in this world is that we each realize that there is more to us than the flesh and bones that make up our physical being, that there is something within each of us well worth loving. It is this love of self which begins the process of transformation in our lives. It is what creates the miracles—the *magic*—the wonder of life.

Magic has been defined as a process to become more than human, to unveil the potential that resides and operates within each of us.

It is not a retreat or escape from life and the turmoils of our daily participation in the life process. Through magic—through opening and expanding our consciousness—we find the means to transmute those turmoils, to change them. We become capable of seeing the turmoils as teachings and thus do what the ancient magicians attempted. We turn the dross of daily life into the gold of greater awareness. Magic is a way of initiating ourselves into a greater awareness that enables our daily life to take on increased radiance.

An occult aphorism states that "Nature unaided fails." Simply, this implies that natural life (and its processes) if left to themselves, isolated and limited by no impact from a higher type of consciousness, will only result in a commonplace thing; or on a more personal level, a commonplace person. The soul by itself if left to itself will eventually seek out its source, but the process can be interminably slow and painstaking. There are means though by which the soul can seek help and assistance in moving along its growth at an accelerated pace. Through higher guidance and expanding awareness we can unfold our soul into another life, a life more filled with love and light. This and this alone is true *magic*.

Still there are those who say that *all* magic is evil. They are qualified to make such statements for they have observed its effects in movies and books which took an ancient and reverent process and perverted it to make money. It is no more evil than the minister who uses his position to increase his own wealth and position. Magic is a technique, and no technique is inherently good or bad. Surgery is also a technique and if abused, it is the man or woman abusing it who is "evil," and not the technique itself. Electricity was once considered the devil's work, but few today would deny its usefulness. Through greater knowledge and familiarity we have been able to harness this mysterious energy called electricity, and through greater knowledge and familiarity we can do the same with true magic.

The word has always held an ancient enchantment for men. It hints of journeys into unseen and unmapped domains. There was a time when the distances between our world and the ones we considered so "magical" were no further than the bend in the road. Each cavern or hollow tree was a doorway to another world where beings existed who evolved side by side with mankind. Man recognized life at all times. The streams spoke and the winds whispered ancient words into the ears of whomever would listen. Every blade of grass and flower had a story to tell. In the blink of an eye, man could explore worlds and seek out knowledge that enlightened his life and his world. Shadows were not just shadows, trees were not just wood and clouds were not just pretty. There was life and purpose in all things, and there was loving interaction between all worlds. Man was only limited by his own fears.

Those fears closed the doors. They silenced the streams and the winds. There was no life but man. Oh sure, there were animals, but that was not life. And the God that created all those worlds and the beauty and love with which they sparkled became hardened in the minds of man. He became vengeful and spiteful, and man forgot how infinitely loving he truly was.

The worlds separated. Man built walls around his cities first and then his mind. His beliefs became restricted and limited. There was no room in it for that which was not logical or rational, and only that which could be experienced by the five senses was rational, and instead of seeking adventures of love and light through all of God's worlds, man searched out the kingdoms of other men. Man did not understand that to a limited mind (to a limited God) jealousy, war and domination would become logical processes in life; the reasons behind them all being very rational.

No world dies. All worlds still exist, though the doorways are now more obscure. Now we must seek them out. There are still noble adventures to undertake. There are pots of gold at the end of rainbows, but now they must be searched out and won. Only through love of the self can this be done. This love is one in which there are no limitations to your world. In a world in which there appear to be infinite problems we must learn that there are also an infinite number of solutions for each one. We are only limited by ourselves.

Above the portals of the ancient Mystery Schools was but one commandment: *"Know thyself."* To know oneself is to love oneself. It is to realize that an infinitely loving God does not forsake His children. In my world there is no room for any other view of God. Through the magic and mysticism of the Qabala, the ancient doors and gates are again opened to each of us. We are offered the opportunity to expand our consciousness that we in turn can radiate more light upon our world.

I have come to realize that thoughts are things

and moods are places. I believe in fairies, pixies, elves, and trees that speak and caverns that lead to nether worlds. I know there are dragons and princesses and wisdom in all things. I have seen Angels, Archangels, devas and celestial beings working with us and for us at all times. My world is full of color and light and *magic*.

To this world you are invited. There are as many ways into it as there are people. All may enter, but enter with reverence and openness, for this also is God's world and those you meet, no matter how they appear, are God's people.

We have all wished for wonderful things in our lives. We've often wondered what it would be like to have that magic wand or find that lamp that holds that powerful genie. It is my hope that through this book, that such possibilities which you can dream of will come that much closer to reality for you. We need only remember: We are never given a dream or a wish without also being given the means and the power to make it manifest. We can each become an instrument capable of using the forces of Light to the dedicated service of God and man. This alone is *magic*.

Chapter 1

The Key

. . . the Qabala opens up access to the occult, to the mysteries. It enables us to read sealed epistles and books and likewise the inner nature of man.

— Paracelsus
(Medieval philosopher,
physician and mystic)

Once upon a time, in the earliest aeons of rational man, there was a young man who was most discontent. Living to work, raise a family and then die did not seem fair to him. In a village that prided itself on its rational and civilized manners, this was quite irrational. After all, of what use was it to work hard and build a good life for one's family and never see the fruits of the labor. Once death arrived, all the work on the physical would certainly be for nothing.

There had to be more to life. There had to be more to the universe than what abided in his village.

1

But no one would help him find the answers. No one wanted to help him search for the answers. It was wrong they said. It was not for man to know the will of God. It was wrong to question! It was wrong to look beyond!

"Why?" he would ask. "Why is it wrong to search? Why was it wrong to question?" After all, he did not want to know the will of God. He merely wanted to know why his life had to be limited by the village and the beliefs that he had inherited from it. Certainly, there had to be more. Why did man have to struggle? Why wasn't man allowed to find joy and enthusiasm for life and in the adventures of life? Why?

But no one answered. No one helped. They were content. Their lives ran smoothly—no matter how boring or limited they might be. They were content, and there was no need to go looking for things that may not exist. There would be no shadow chasing for them. Oh, there might be some wonderful things out there in the universe somewhere, but there could also be some not-so-wonderful things as well. Best to leave well enough alone. Best to be content with what is at hand.

Curiosity and the promise of dreams were strong within the boy, and he set out in search of answers. He learned of a wise old man who inhabited a cave at the crest of a distant mountain. The man was rumor and legend, but as with all myths, the boy knew there were elements of truth within it.

After many days of long climbs he reached the crest of the mountain, and from this point he could see the towns and villages and valleys and farms of what looked to be the whole world, and he smiled. Surely, this is the place a man of wisdom would choose to live!

As he turned from his view to seek out his teacher, he spied a small cottage in the distance. Beside the cottage was a small garden being tended by an old man. As the boy approached, his spirits fell and his heart again ached. Before him was an old man, but the old man was just that. There was no light about him. There was no glow, no power that surely would emanate from a true man of wisdom. There was none of this about the old man. He was worn and wrinkled and looked like nothing but a farmer.

The old man smiled and nodded in warm greeting and the boy could not help but return the smile. At least he could refresh himself here. The old man lay down his hoe and sat himself upon a tree stump across from the boy.

"What is it you seek, lad?"

The boy sighed. "I had hoped to find an answer."

"I am not without a little bit of knowledge, perhaps I can help you."

"I don't think so. I don't need to know of farming or tending gardens. The answers I seek are more. I seek to know the answer to the universe. I want to know why man must struggle. I want to know why man cannot have what he dreams of. I want to know why birds can fly and man can't. After all, are we not so much better than the beasts of the air? I want to know . . . ?"

The boy rattled on, citing question after question. He didn't know why he told all to this man, but he did. And the grizzled old man sat and listened patiently, nodding now and again, but saying nothing.

The boy's words became interspersed with yawns as the weariness of his journey and climb began to catch up with him. He did not know when exactly, but sometime during his talking, he drifted off to sleep. It was deep and long, and when he awoke, he was refreshed.

He stretched and stood and then stopped in surprise. The old man was gone! And so were the cottage and the garden! He spun around, looking in all directions, confused and bewildered. Had he dreamed it all? Had he imagined it all?

All that remained was the tree stump. Upon the stump were two scrolls. The boy picked them up gently and glanced about him as if someone were watching from behind a bush. There was no one. He unrolled a scroll and read:

> Son,
>
> There is much to learn and an eternity to learn it, but before we can learn the new, we must unlearn the old. Hold on to your questions, for with the asking of the question we have the beginning of the answer.
>
> To you I bequeath this second scroll. It is a map of the universe and all that resides within and without it. You may notice that it appears quite simple, but this is the first that must be unlearned. It is in the simple that the great can be found. Intricacies complicate and confuse.
>
> Build your universe from a simple and

yet strong foundation. You are surprised that I say "build." But that is what you will be doing, for as you discover the universe, you will recreate your own.

You will notice that the directions are simple and rational, a term you disfavor, but it must be. As much as you disfavor the rational, it is a part of your makeup. It is a tool with which you will be able to grow and understand. Remember that it is only in its unbalanced state that the world becomes barren.

Be true to yourself and to the knowledge contained herein. Herein lies the foundation to live in light, grow in wisdom and express with love. It is for you as it is for all mankind who wish to remove their self-imposed blinders and discover the Hidden Light behind all lights.

> In Love and Brotherhood,
> Your First Answer

Overwhelmed, the boy sat down and began to read the second scroll. He savored it; he studied it and time lost all meaning. He now stood upon the brink of a new world. He had found what had been hidden . . .

(To be continued)

Mention the word "occult" and people call to mind images of spell casting, devil worship, Halloween, evil witchcraft and bizarre happenings behind closed doors. To mention that you are a student of the occult is to invite an often rude awakening as to whom your true friends are. In reality, it is merely a six-letter word, derived from the Greek language, meaning "hidden." It refers to the hidden knowledge, mysteries and truths of God and life. It is neither sinful nor demonic in itself. It is simply veiled knowledge, so as to allow man the opportunity to seek and grow and mature enough to use it responsibly in its highest capacity.

There are those who argue that such knowledge is hidden and obscured because God does not want man to discover it. If that were the case, the alphabet, algebra and electricity would be just as "demonic" as other so-called "occult" ideas and truths. They were understood by relatively few, but no one today would deny their usefulness. The Master Jesus stated, "Things are hidden only to be revealed at a later time." (Mark 4:22). The knowledge is obscure because the majority refuses the discipline and dedication necessary to seek it out, much less to attempt an understanding of it.

It is unfortunate that the term has acquired such a strong, negative connotation. There are now those who attribute any outbreak of trouble to that unknown nemesis known as the "occult." When there is disruption or disintegration in the ranks of religious groups, it must either be an occult attack from outside the group or the retaliation of some "occult" forces of evil with which they have been waging daring battles. It is the stuff of fiction!

Mankind has made great progress technologically.

Physically, we are stronger and healthier. Mentally we are sharper and expanding, but spiritually as a whole we are stagnant. Our knowledge has outstripped our spiritual teachings. They are growing incompatible. Without expansion of our spiritual understanding, the gap can only widen. Simple conformity with approved theological institutions no longer satisfies. There is an increasing need for a more personal and complete, spiritual experience.

All major religions teach that we are to return to some "primal point" from which we came. Some call this heaven, some *nirvana*. This ultimate of experiences is called Divine Union, but other than teaching church doctrines and moral codes, the major religions are not teaching the extent to which we can manifest this link while in the physical. They do not teach the extent to which we progress through a *natural* course of evolvement—as if progressing through a school—accumulating greater skills, abilities and knowledge to assist us in our life. They do not teach the practical means to enhance and accelerate this natural course of evolvement, of expanding our spiritual knowledge and applying it to all aspects of life. They do not teach how to make use of the so-called metaphysical gifts as a working aspect of our daily life.

In every person, the qualities essential for accelerating this spiritual evolution are innate. Within each of us are gifts and potentials that we can use to enhance our lives. Whether we call these psychic gifts, metaphysical powers, miracles of life, or spiritual wonders does not matter. They exist within each of us, but even people who recognize these potentials need an effective means of unfolding them. There needs to be a system that allows us to recognize and then utilize all of the spiritual potential within us.

For any such system to be of true benefit to all, it must be easily understood—at least in its most basic form and conception. It must be a living and growing system that allows itself to be adapted to each individual and his or her particular stage of unfoldment while holding its basic, primary form and content. It should awaken our inherent abilities and open the doors to our higher consciousness. It should enable us to feel and experience increasingly the universal forces operating within it. The practices, energies and forces within the system should be such that they can be experienced in a manner that encourages continued pursuit, inspiration and exploration throughout its use.

The mystical Qabala is just such a system. It is one of the most esoteric, occult and yet practical systems for expanding our consciousness and unfolding our spiritual gifts and awareness. It has been called the Western Tradition of Occultism, and within it lies the Wisdom of the Ancients and all of the powers of the universe. Within it lies the means to contact those divine powers and be touched by them. Through it, one can go as far and as deeply into the mysteries of life as one desires. It is especially suited to the rational Western mind because it is a system that allows us to see some organization of the powers and energies of the universe and how they play upon each of us as individuals and as a group.

Qabala comes from the ancient word *qibel* which

means "to receive" or "that which is received." In the ancient world it had a more general meaning of "the Law." It is the earliest form of Jewish mysticism. There are many stories of how it came to be. Most claim that it was the knowledge given to Moses on Mount Sinai during the episode of the burning bush. Another version says that it was taught by God to the Angels who formed a school based upon it in paradise. After man's fall, the Angels passed it on to the children of the Earth so that they may again overcome the earth plane and ascend to the heavens.

It is told that the Archangel Metatron gave the Qabala to Adam who in turn passed it on down to Noah and then to Abraham. When Abraham emigrated to Egypt, a portion of it leaked out. Thus the Egyptians obtained greater spiritual and mystical knowledge (along with other Eastern nations) which assisted them in establishing one of the greatest civilizations in the history of mankind.

In this version, Moses, who was first initiated into its uses by the Egyptians, became quite proficient in it during the forty years upon the desert. Tradition states that during this time he received more instruction in it from the Angels and used it to ovecome many of the difficulties in the desert. The "mannah from heaven" is attributed to his knowledge of the Qabala. He passed it on to the elders who in turn passed it on from generation to generation by word of mouth. David and Solomon were probably the most deeply initiated into its wisdom and mysteries.

The modern Qabala is a mixture of the Jewish Qabala and the core ideas of the most ancient Egyptian religion which led to illumination. It has been found in the Chaldean religion. It was a part of the teachings of Pythagoras, and Jesus made numerous references to it. The phrasing of the Lord's Prayer is very Qabalistic in itself.

Even with its ancient origins it is still a very living system of evolvement. Its uses and interpretations vary, expand and adapt from generation to generation. Its foundations are firm, but its uses involve changes that meet and coordinate with the outside world. It is a changing system, but changing only in that it grows and expands. Since there can be no growth without change, this is quite appropriate. It is studied and used to initiate change within ourselves and thus also within our environment. Change does not come from life itself, but from living that life and by acting upon and within it. The Qabala assists in this.

Today's student of the Qabala must reinterpret the doctrines and reformulate methods in the light of modern knowledge if it is to be of use. The purity of a tradition or idea must be tested if it is to have any life in it. Dead doctrines and faith never insure belief. Tradition is fine, but to let it rule to the exclusion of new growth is a denial of the basic tenets of a *living* system. Any tree is a living, growing thing, and if alive, implied within it is change. All tools and teachings are capable of being changed and extended beyond their first applications.

The Qabala is a plan for a flower garden. Provided are the tools, the tasks, the sunshine, the water, the fertilizer, and seed enough for infinite plant life.

Provided are the instructions and procedures for the planting, hoeing and harvesting. But with all this, the actual working is up to the individual. No other system is as complete in providing the energy, inspiration, confirmation and greater realization of mystical experience. It will even go so far as to point out where the weeds are, but the task of pulling them is still ours. That choice is always ours.

"We are the masters of our own destiny." Working with the Qabala makes this absolutely clear. When working with the Qabala, you must be careful what you ask, for you will get it! It demonstrates on all levels of our life that we are the authors of all our experiences, from the non-accident of birth, to the parents we chose, the environment in which we now live, and the time and circumstances of our own death. We write the scripts. This is not an easy concept to accept for it lays the responsibility for everything that occurs in our lives on us—and only us! If you are not ready to accept the responsibility for where you are now and where you want to be, the Qabala will make it quite evident. It will open new worlds and new wonders. It will show you your greatest dreams and potentials. It will make you face your greatest fears and darkest secrets.

As children, we had very few limitations in our life. We experienced realities which we closed down as we got older. The openness of that child is still within us. It's what makes us dream of that magic wand which will make all our troubles disappear and create new wonders and beauty within our world. That wand is out there, but we have to search it out.

The Qabala shows us where to look.

> "Know what it is to be a child? . . .It is to be
> so little that the elves can reach to whisper
> in your ear. It is to turn pumpkins into
> coaches and mice into horses . . . for each
> child has his fairy Godmother within his
> own soul."
>
> —Fr. Francis Thompson

Chapter 2

The Tree of Life

As above, so below.
> —Principle of Correspondence
> from the Emerald Tablet
> of Hermes Trismegistus

*And God said, 'Let us make man in our
own image and after our own likeness . . .*
> —Genesis 1:26

*The second star to the right and straight on
'til morning.*
> —Peter Pan

When we were children, we longed for adventure.
There was excitement and wonder all about us. That
first trip to the zoo opened our eyes to life and worlds
we had not even imagined. Each animal was strange
and new and captivating. Each day offered new adventures and new wonders to behold. Everything and

everyone was special. Anything we could imagine was real to us, be it ghost or space ship or fairies or pirates. We could be anything we wanted, explore every nook and cranny within the world. Time was inconsequential. We could be Indians in the morning and be searching out buried treasures in the afternoon. There were no limits, no borders. Each day was a myriad of rainbow-hued metamorphoses.

That ability to see the sparkle of the world as if for the first time is still within each of us. Our lives should still be filled with that same wide-eyed wonder and thrill that we experienced in our youth. It only passes from us if we allow it. It is not out of reach. It can be rediscovered. There are still buried treasures to be found. There are worlds to be explored. There is adventure and joy and magic to fill our lives and awaken our souls.

The Qabala is like a map. It is a map to buried treasures within our mind. It leads to hidden lands within our consciousness where we can find treasures and wonders to enhance and fulfill our lives.

We must bear in mind that the Qabala is dual in nature. It is a map of how the universe itself was formed and manifested, and it is also a map of how the forces of the universe manifest in each one of us *without exception*. With the infinite energies, powers, forces and life forms abounding within the universe, it is very necessary that we have some means of organizing, distinguishing and placing them in a context in which we can begin to explore them. As we begin to search them out, we increase our own understanding and discover how they operate within our own lives.

The Qabala is our treasure map. It provides the best means for Westerners to discover the wonders that exist within each one of us. It leads to the gifts and abilities that make our lives a joy and an adventure. It provides the best means for us to progress and evolve spiritually. We in the West are more rational minded than our Eastern counterparts. We are raised and fed rational organization. We tend to employ greater left-brain activity within our lives. The Qabala allows us to do this to our advantage, for while it appeases that rational aspect within us, it also awakens and stimulates greater right-brain activity. It leads us to greater intuitive and creative activity within our lives.

The Qabala gives us a systematic and logical view of the universe, its evolution and the energies within it. This enables us then to focus those energies more creatively to our benefit. It guides us to those abilities within us that allow greater creative capacities to manifest.

The Qabala has traditionally been presented as mysterious and complex. It appears to have so many ideas, forces, correlations and applications that it frustrates the beginner. But we must remember that it is only a map, and for the beginner it is always best to stay on the main trails until we are familiar with them. Then we can explore the other routes. The map is only difficult to follow if we try to take on more than we are capable of.

We would no more expect a fifth grader to take a class in advanced physics any more than the beginner to the Qabala should be expected to learn all the routes and paths upon the map. Within this map is also the treasure of understanding ourselves on all levels: physical, emotional, mental and spiritual. It is simply an attempt to put in diagram form every force, form and factor within the universe and within the soul of man.

What is most wonderful about this map that we call the Qabalistic Tree of Life is that it adapts itself to every individual. It only gets as complicated and involved as we allow it. That in itself is magical! It allows us to seek out the treasures and worlds of wonder at our own speed. It allows us to learn and grow at our own rate. We can each take the routes and seek out the treasures that are most suitable to us. We can follow it in as safe or as adventuresome a manner as we are capable. No matter how we follow the map, it will lead to those treasures within!

The Tree of Life is deceptively simple. It is a *living* symbol in that all of the forces represented are alive and acting upon us at all times. Nothing operates within the universe without affecting something else. The raising of an arm may be thought a single act, but it involves many factors: brain waves, nerve impulses, muscle contraction, etc. Everything operates in relation to something else. We cannot entirely separate one aspect from the other. Thus by working with this map we begin to recognize and understand about the forces operating within our life and so learn to balance and use them to our advantage and growth, rather than being at their mercy.

Man is a miniature universe. In other words, those forces and factors which make up the manifested universe on all levels are also present within the nature of man *without exception*. The symbol of the Tree of Life is the epitome of the microcosmic/macrocosmic view of the universe. By learning to awaken and apply the forces symbolized within it, we are able to touch and awaken greater spheres of our own inner nature. Thus, on the one hand, while the forces and powers within the Tree represent successive phases of evolution within the universe, on the other hand they also represent successive levels of greater consciousness and energies within each one of us. The idea behind working with the Tree is to expand our awareness of the universe and to awaken our consciousness to the energies and forces that exist simultaneously within it and us. We, in fact, through study, meditation and various simple exercises can become a living Tree of Life, replete with all the inherent forces and energies of the universe and the potential to connect with everything else in the universe. We have our roots upon the Earth and our head in the Heavens, and circulating throughout us, for us, are all the forces of the universe. To some this is magic, but it is really nothing more than life itself.

In the beginning there was Nothingness. To the Qabalist, its various degrees are referred to as Ain, Ain Soph and Ain Soph Aur (see Figure One). To the ordinary person, this simply refers to the fact that there is a point in divine spiritual matters that is entirely beyond our understanding—at least as long as we are in physical form. This Nothingness is comprised of all the energies and forces of the Divine Universe, existing in a harmony beyond our understanding at a time before our existence. It is that

NOTHINGNESS—Primal Point from which we came and to which we return, beyond understanding.

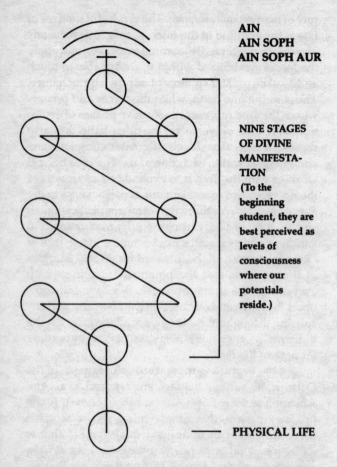

AIN
AIN SOPH
AIN SOPH AUR

NINE STAGES
OF DIVINE
MANIFESTA-
TION
(To the
beginning
student, they are
best perceived as
levels of
consciousness
where our
potentials
reside.)

PHYSICAL LIFE

Figure One. The Path of the Flaming Sword is the path that Divine Spirit took through nine stages of manifestation before finally densifying and manifesting into physical life as we know it.

"primal point" from which we came and to which we will someday return. The act of creation—the act of Divine Spirit manifesting from a state beyond physical reality (and thus beyond entire comprehension, i.e. Nothingness) as seen within the Qabala—provides a way of perceiving how we can each evolve and attain to higher and greater gifts.

The Divine Spirit began to manifest through stages, its energies acquiring greater density, much in the same manner as steam can condense into water and then into ice. Everything is energy at some level or another. The electrons and protons that make up every atom of every substance and form have motion. As they compact together, we have different forms and stages of manifested energy.

The energy came forth from the Nothingness, densifying through stages. It followed a specific manner—grouping, expanding, restricting, overflowing—through nine stages of manifestation, until these energies densified into physical. The physical universe was the tenth and final stage. Each stage came from that which was before it and gave birth to all that followed. Thus within each stage of evolution was the seed of all the energies and forces which came before. Each stage just became a more specific aspect of the All Energy. Each stage was new in its own specific direction and application of the original, and yet the same as the original in that it contained aspects of what came before. Each stage was a further focusing and delineating of the divine universal energy from which everything came. Each stage was a branch off the same tree, but each branch was capable of bearing its own fruit. Each was unique in that it was more focused than what came before and yet the same in that the sap (the life force) running throuogh it is that which runs through them all.

Thus the Tree of Life is a manner of classifying the energies and organizing them so that they are more workable to the Western mind. It provides a manner of understanding and achieving perspective of how the universe and everything inherent within it exists within each of us. When we see how the Divine manifests through us, we can then begin to manifest our own abilities and potentials more actively within our lives.

It must be remembered throughout this that the Qabala is not a religion nor philosophy per se. It contains *aspects* of many religions and philosophies. It is simply a way of working with and increasing our understanding of our own potential and gifts. By doing so we can then begin to use them more creatively and more positively within our lives. We make our lives more balanced and more fruitful. If this is hocus pocus to some, so be it, but anything that raises the quality and spirituality of life is well worth exploring. The study of the Tree of Life enables us to do this. We begin to again take more control of our course of evolvement. We take the responsibility back. Our lives and our futures then are not left to chance or to some harsh and stern conception of the Divine.

The Tree of Life consists of ten *spheres* called the Ten Holy Sephiroth with 22 lines connecting the different spheres. These connecting lines are called *paths*, and together with the Ten Holy Sephiroth they make up what are called the 32 Paths of Wisdom. These 32 paths are doorways of experience to greater spiritual awareness and evolvement. We must keep in mind that each sphere is essentially a level of consciousness that resides within us. Each is a level wherein are many of our hidden abilities and potentials. The sephiroth then are actual states of consciousness wherein forces and abilities of each of us operate. The paths connecting the sephiroth are steps by which we can reach those levels of consciousness. They are the steps by which we unfold and reawaken a greater realization of the universe and our individual places within it. This is called "Awakening the God-Spark."

Each sephira is dual in nature. They each represent a stage in the manifestation of Divine Spirit into the universe, i.e. the creative process. They each also represent levels of consciousness within us. As each sephira established itself with all of its energies and forces it then overflowed to form the next at a denser level. This sequential evolvement is called the Path of the Flaming Sword. Meditation upon this title in relation to the entire process will yield a great deal of information to the student. The evolution then ended in Malkuth, the center of all physical existence as we know it including man. Thus, Malkuth and man alike are the recipients of all the forces and energies of the Divine.

At this point it becomes the responsibility of each individual to reawaken those forces. This is done by work and exercises at *each* level of consciousness. Each time we touch one of these levels, more of the innate energy and awareness is awakened within us.

By touching and utilizing those energies in a balanced manner within our life, we work our way up the path of spiritual evolution. This is what flames the God-Spark within each of us. This is where the magic and miracles begin. Each time we climb the Tree, each time we touch more deeply one of the levels of consciousness, we become a brighter light within the world. And that is what makes life exciting and joyous and fun! This is the buried treasure to which the map leads us Each level of consciousness contains a treasure chest of gold and jewels and wealth to add sparkle and brilliance to our lives.

Chapter 3

The Powers That Be

Behold, thy soul is a living star!
          —Egyptian Book of the Dead

Each sephira is a level of consciousness wherein resides certain capabilities, energies and potentials. The Qabala provides a system for understanding the various energies at those levels. Each of these levels in turn have various depths where the energies reside. The more we then work with them, the more they reveal to us. It can be like a surprise Christmas present where the box that holds the gift actually contains more boxes and gifts than what appeared at first. The greatest gifts are always those which are more than we ever expected!

We must bear in mind that the formation of the universe (from pure spiritual energy to physical matter) is distinguished as different stages. We recognize them initially as separate forces and powers. This enables us to apply them more easily to our lives, but we must remember that they are not truly separate and distinct energies. They are simply different aspects of the same universal energy just as water, steam and ice are different aspects of the same elements. By initially treating them as separate levels of consciousness it is easier for us to work with them. There comes a point though within our work and our evolvement when we realize that within each of us is the power equivalent to any within the universe.

The Qabala is a system for expanding our consciousness and awareness and for accelerating our own growth. When we first work with the sephiroth, we simply try to get a picture, an overview, of the energy and power that thrives at that level of consciousness within us. Ultimately, we are attempting to see this energy as a very active and real aspect of our own world: our own being. We are trying to experience it as an actual part of our lives. These energies that reside at those levels within us are neither imaginary nor simply of the mind. They are as real as every other aspect of our being. We don't see the energy that pumps our blood, but we know it is there. In essence it is the same energy that moves the planets and stars, only working on a more minute and less grandiose manner. The sephiroth reveal the nature of physical and psychical phenomena, and once understood, we can use those same principles to exercise control over life's conditions and circumstances.

Each level of consciousness within us has principal ideas/energies associated with them. They are given to us in the form of symbols. The symbols open the doors to the various levels (i.e. sephiroth) within us. Keep in mind that each person's map is individual. Although all have some basic foundations, they are all living and growing maps, adapting themselves to your own rate of growth and particular stage of evolvement. This means we should not limit ourselves to just the principal ideas associated with each level. As we each use the map, we may find correspondences, relationships and treasures that may not be similar to someone else's. That is perfectly fine because we all follow the map according to our own capabilities and needs. Thus, we awaken and use those aspects most suitable to our own growth. We can use the basic principles as guideposts so that we don't get lost, but by no means should we limit ourselves to that. The Tree of Life represents universal forces operating on many levels and is constantly in motion. It is a living, changing map.

The energies, and the symbols used to express them at a particular state of consciousness, encompass many aspects. For this reason, as we grow and change, adding greater depth to our life, so will the sephiroth change revealing greater depths and treasures. For this reason we should seek to find in each sephira that which most corresponds to us as individuals, and to our world.

Each sephira has its own facets, its own individual ways in which its energies can be found and expressed. There are many principal symbols associated with these energies. Meditation, contemplation, reverie surrounding any one of them opens the doors to that level of our consciousness. This book will focus only on the major associations with each. The first is the *title*

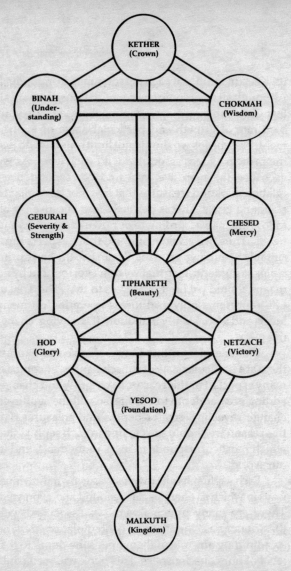

Figure Two. The ten sephiroth (the ten levels of conscious-ness) within the map of the Tree of Life and the titles that reflect the character of the energy found at that level.

of the sephira which reveals the principal force that the sephira contains. Next will be the *God Name:* a name of tremendous power representing the highest spiritual force within that sephira. Next will be the *Archangels* and *Angels*, the highest form of life encountered at those levels, and then there will be discussed other important aspects of the energy found in that sephira. Remember that, even though the sephira may be described as if it were a place, for the beginner it is best to look upon it as a *state of consciousness within ourselves*.

As mentioned, each sephira is assigned a title. This title indicates the primary idea, principle or energy associated with the sephiroth. Just as various cities or countries have a "nickname" that reflects their character, so do the sephiroth (see Figure Two).

Each sephira has a Divine Name, a God Name. All of the God Names are actually divine aspects of the One God, the one universal power that encompasses all powers. This is the supreme Name of Power, ruling that level of consciousness, and it represents the most spiritual form of the force within us at that level. It is the most powerful aspect at that level and dominates all other aspects. The names render much in meditation and they are well worth exploring. They can also be used as powerful mantrams and this is explored in a later chapter. It represents the purest form of the energy at that level, so care should be taken in its use or when concentrating upon it for the purpose of invocation and awakening. It could prove too hot to handle, especially in the beginning.

Even when working with other aspects of the sephira, the Divine Name should still be considered

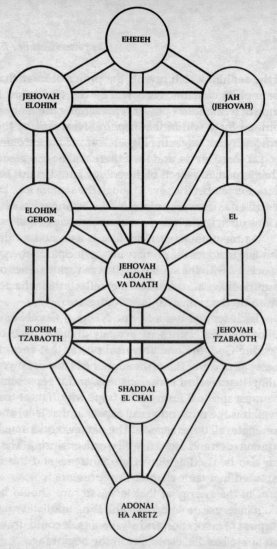

Figure Three. The God Names associated with each level. This is the supreme spiritual power available to you at the level in which you are working. It is much more effective to use these than a generic title such as "God."

first. It is a well-understood, ancient principle that all things come first from the spiritual. Thus, always invoke the aid of the God Name first before focusing on the other aspects of the sephira. A simple prayer for guidance and protection that employs the God Name is quite easy and effective. It is much more effective than just calling upon a generic title such as God (see Figure Three).

To each sephira is assigned an Archangel and an Order of Angels. They are there to guide us and protect us and teach us about the energies associated with that particular level. Most people relegate these magnificent beings to the realm of fiction and fairy tales, especially in this age of intellectual and scientific pursuit. One cannot work with the Qabala however, and not realize just how very real and loving they are. If for no other reason than to realize the reality of these celestial beings, the Qabala is well worth the study. One's life will never be the same!

They are just as real as any of us, but without physical bodies. They have bodies of lighter substance that are mostly invisible to our self-limiting perceptions. We exist in a living universe, and there is life and energy in all we see, and refuse to see. Much of the good we know, be it the beauty of nature or the gift of birth or any of the wonders and blessings of life, we owe to them.

Humans are smug. We like to believe we are the highest form of life. We do have a Divine Spark, and we are heirs to all the forces and energies of the universe, but so are countless numbers of other life forms. And there are many more that express that

Divine Spark much more radiantly and much more consistently than we do. Even the lowest Angel is more highly evolved than an uninitiated man or woman.

Angels are beings capable of disseminating the light of God to all religions and all lives created by God. They number myriad upon myriad and they serve every function imaginable. They form a very important aspect of the Qabala, but they are by no means limited to it and to those who work with it. Through the Qabala we have the means to work with them more directly. Our consciousness is broadened by considering the existence of lives unlike us in physical apearance but one with us in service to God. We need to develop our awareness and respect for them and their office. The Qabala assists. By working with them and recognizing their works, we extend and heighten our own Divine Spark and increase the recognition of God's Universal Light within our lives and our world.

We are whole beings now, but we must accept that we are. This is why we work with the Qabala. We've had many way-showers, great teachers who have walked the Earth, and from each of them we can learn and grow, but we do not have to limit ourselves to them! The Angels, from their vantage point and from their willing and loving interplay with the various levels of our own consciousness, can assist us in connecting more quickly with our divine origin and make our steps so much easier. The angelic beings will assist each and every one of us to be initiated into any and all the mysteries and wonders of life, but we first must learn to reverence *all* life that surrounds us on all planes and all levels of awareness. The wonders and miracles of life—both physical and spiritual—are ours to be enjoyed, but only after our reverence and love for that supreme Spirit includes both the visible and invisible realms of life.

The Archangels are real. It is much easier to work with them rather than with the God Names. The archangelic energy is much easier to handle because it is a little bit closer to the density of physical energy. The Archangels are very individual, intelligent and purposeful. One of the supreme pleasures and joys of working with the Qabala is the contact that it establishes with these beings. They demonstrate wisdom, strength of will and love that is totally unconditional, and to receive their assistance is no more difficult than requesting it.

Working with the Archangels in each sephira is a specific Order of Angels. They represent intelligent, natural forces and are responsible for the mechanics of the energy flow at each level. They work with how the energy in that sephira manifests. While the Archangels organize the energies and forces for our use in the sephiroth, the Order of Angels see to the working of that organization.

The Angels associated with the sephira are by no means the only Angels. They are simply the ones working with the forces and energies available to us at those levels. There are other Orders of Angels—beautiful and great—who work in other arenas of life.

The Angels form a link between us and the Divine. When trying to contact them, all we need do is imagine

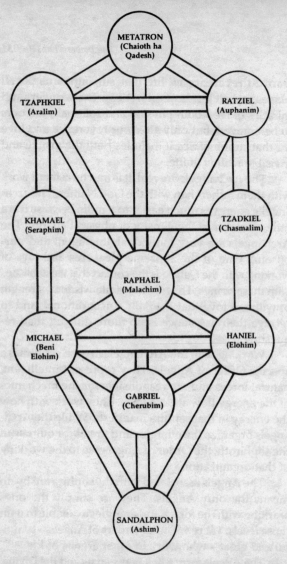

Figure Four. The archangelic and angelic beings to which we have greater access and can meet and work with more directly at each level of consciousness.

them as they are: beautiful beings of light and glory; deep, protective presences. They impress us and inspire us. They show us how to realize what we are. They execute their tasks with a creative joy and resourcefulness and color that is beyond our own labors. They demonstrate that there is no drudgery in any task, for all have their places in the scheme of evolvement (see Figure Four).

The next association or energy found within the sephiroth is called the mundane chakra. This represents a more physical aspect of the energy. In simple terms, it is the form of energy we feel most directly in the physical. To symbolize this, each level of consciousness is given a planetary association. This is primarily an astrological attribution, and a study of astrology will render an understanding of the type of effect the energy within that sephira can have. This is not to say that the planets do or do not affect us, but rather that the energies that we associate with the planets in astrology are found at these levels.

For most of the sephiroth, there is also a vice and a virtue. They are not truly a part of the sephiroth or found at those levels of consciousness. They do indicate though how we might respond to the energy at that level when we tap it. The virtue is the quality most essential to working with the forces of the sephiroth. It also indicates the gift that these forces can bring to your growth. The vice is an imbalance of the force of the sephiroth. It is an imbalance that the forces of the sephiroth can cause through our own natural weakness. As was stated earlier, the Qabala will show us our greatest dreams and potentials, but it will also

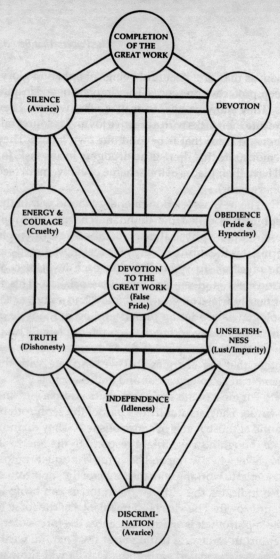

Figure Five. The virtues and the vices (in parentheses) and their relative energies that exist at each level which we can tap and utilize to overcome weaknesses and enhance growth.

make us face our greatest fears and darkest secrets. We must keep in mind that no level of consciousness is either virtuous or vice-ridden in itself. They each contain universal force—*neutral and unconditional*. How we awaken it and use it determines its worth. Imbalances show us our human weaknesses so that we can attempt to overcome them and evolve.

There are many other associations with the sephiroth. To each are assigned incenses, precious and semi-precious stones, parts of the physical body, geometric figures, numbers, Hebrew letters, mythological gods and goddesses, astrological symbolism, tarot cards and colors. All simply help us to understand more of the energy and force at the various levels. All are simply other doorways to enter the various levels, but they are not necessary for those just beginning their work—those just opening the doors to their own worlds of treasure and delight.

Chapter 4

Destination's End

*. . . And here were gardens bright with
 sinuous rills,
Where blossomed many an incense-
 bearing tree,
And here were forests ancient as the hills,
Enfolding sunny spots of greenery . . .*
—Samuel Taylor Coleridge

When we begin a new journey, it is always best to know something about our destination. We need to know what to expect. We need to know what to look for. We need to be able to recognize when we are there. By knowing something about the various levels of consciousness, the powers that reside there and what potentials they can awaken within us, we are able to focus our attention more directly and learn to discriminate from that which is beneficial and that which is not. It is easy to become confused and somewhat disoriented at various levels of our consciousness, but if we have become familiar with a general description of them then we can insure that we have not gotten lost in the process. When entering any new territory, it is always best to be somewhat familiar with the terrain.

As we work with the sephiroth as states of consciousness, it will gradually unfold to us that they are also actual planes of existence where there is life just as real as life in the physical. At this point we need to remember that the purpose of following the Qabala is to expand our consciousness and our awareness, to begin to remove the blinders and limitations that we have imposed upon ourselves. We are trying to realize the reality of life existing in all degrees and on all planes. This is why one of the most joyful, most blessed and most unforgettable experiences is that first contact with the angelic life operating within the sephiroth. The wisdom, love and power that they evoke touches you in a manner that carries over to the physical realms. It drives home the fact that there are beings of finer substance willing to lovingly help us in our growth in spite of ourselves.

As we examine the terrain within the levels of consciousness that we call the sephiroth, we will not look at them in the order in which they manifested. When we begin to work with them and follow our own maps, we should do so *in reverse order*, starting with the level of Malkuth. These levels closest to Malkuth are the ones closest to our own normal state of consciousness. As we move up the Tree, the levels become more spiritual in their nature. That does not make them better or more powerful than the others, just a level at which it is more difficult for us to handle and awaken while we are still in the physical ourselves. It is difficult to change steam into ice instantly. It is much easier to do so in stages, allowing it to condense into water and then into ice. As we will discover, it takes very little to awaken the energies at the various levels. Concentration and focus opens the doors. If we have not prepared ourselves sufficiently, the energy will be disturbing and very unsettling. It would be like trying to run 600 volts of electricity through a 110 volt outlet or wire.

MALKUTH

Malkuth is that temple of consciousness closest to our natural waking conscious. It is the level that most directly affects physical life. Malkuth, although located at the bottom of our map, is of no less importance than any of the other levels of consciousness. It is, in fact, the recipient of *all* the energies from *all* the other levels. It is thus our task to begin to recognize, separate and utilize those energies to their fullest extent.

It is this level of consciousness that we are able to touch that aspect of the Divine, called Adonai Ha-Aretz (AH-DOH-NI HAH-AH-RATZ) or Lord of the Earth and the Visible Universe. This is the God of the kingdom of man and has the most direct influence in our physical and material affairs.

There are, in fact, several Archangels that can be contacted in this level of consciousness. For the beginner, the easiest and the most readily available will be Sandalphon. He is known as the Approacher and the Prince of Prayer, for it is he who will take our prayers to where they can best be answered. He is also instrumental in bringing about the differentiation of sex within the embryo and holds a strong hand in the formation of all physical life. He gathers the prayers of the faithful and delivers them personally to the King of Kings. He is often thought to have walked the earth plane himself as the prophet Elijah, and it is through his intercession that we contact the other two Archangels associated with this sphere: Metatron and he whom we call the Holy Spirit.

Working under Sandalphon in the level of Malkuth are the Ashim or the Souls and Flames of Fire. In simple terms, they are the saints most closely aligned with the earth plane. They are the Order of Blessed Souls.

At this level, we can begin to recognize the Divinity that resides within all physical matter. We can come to recognize the life that exists around us—life that has its own consciousness. It is in this level that we can begin to work with devic beings and learn the realities of elemental life. The group that has had such success with contacting and working with the devas for the promulgation of the Earth at Findhorn are doing so primarily through this level of consciousness. Their success should serve to remind us all that we have resources available to each that go untouched. The earthen colors of this sphere, olive, russet, citrines, remind us of the connection.

The vice of this sphere than can be awakened within us and which we enter this level to overcome is that of *inertia* or *avarice*. We are on the physical plane and so if we are to produce the fruit, we must labor for it. There are those that will take their labors to extremes which leads to the avarice aspect.

We work at this level to awaken greater discrimination within our lives. That is the virtue that we can uncover for ourselves here. We learn to discriminate between what is good, what is bad, where to move, where not to move, when to work, when to rest. Learning to discriminate and discover what is best for *you* as an individual is why we utilize this level. By doing so, we can then experience or begin to experience what is called, "The Vision of the Holy Guardian Angel." This is our inner selves, our greater selves, that which is hidden within our physical shells. This level of consciousness reveals to us those things hidden within our physical world or universe. It reveals to us those things hidden within our physical world or universe. It reveals to us those things which we have trained ourselves to ignore or relegate to fancy and fantasy. This is the level wherein we can learn the realities of those we call "fairies" and the reality of the divine potentials within ourselves.

YESOD

Yesod is that level of consciousness associated with the Moon. Deep violets fill this level. It is the Foundation of the astral and etheric planes of life. It is that level in which our mind can build the images that connect us to all others in our life. Through this level we can increase our understanding of the rhythms, fluctuations and tides of organic growth and cyclic changes going on around us. It is here that we can touch our subconscious, psychic and biological functions of life and awaken and stimulate them into greater activity. It is at this level that we can build thought-forms and images that will pull increasing energy from the other levels.

The aspect of God that operates at this level more strongly than any other is called Shaddai El Chai (SHAH-DI-EL-KI), or the Almighty Living God. Touching this aspect at this level, we experience what is called a Vision of the Machinery of the Universe. This does not mean that we will understand the divine plan behind all things, but rather that we are moving forward and as we continue to do so, we realize that the plan or reasoning will be revealed in their own time. This experience is very comforting in itself. It awakens and strengthens our independence. At this level we begin to learn to be more independent based on what we already know and can thus—through this level— begin to synthesize. This level of consciousness assists us in allowing the independence of others as well.

If unbalanced, what will be awakened through this sphere is idleness. Idleness, in that we become content with what we have found and utilized at this level (such as greater psychism and intuition) from the hard work and effort that we have put forth up to this time and we feel no more need to move on. It is then that we must again work with the previous level of consciousness and strengthen our discrimination ability.

Gabriel is the Archangel that we may meet through this level. He is the Angel of Truth and is the chief of guards placed over Paradise. This is appropriate in that the level of Yesod is the gateway to all the other levels of consciousness available to us. He brings us the gift of hope and the reason for having it, no matter the circumstances.

The Cherubim work with them, and if we touch this level, we will contact them as well. They are the Angels of Light and Glory and the Keepers of the Celestial Records. These are most often referred to as the akashic records. These contain all the information on any person or situation; past, present and future. They excel in knowledge and by learning to touch and work with them at this level, we can have greater knowledge from these records made available to us.

HOD

Hod is the orange level of consciousness. It is called Glory. It corresponds to the sphere of Mercury in astrology. Working in this level assists us in books and learnings, communications, trade, commerce, and the exchange of ideas. This level can reveal insight into travel, contracts, the art of magic and of thought in general. It is in this sphere, this level of consciousness, that we can learn to imprint our will upon astral matter in order to create greater manifestations within physical life. It is here that one can learn about materialization and dematerialization.

The God aspect that operates at this level of consciousness most strongly is called Elohim Tzabaoth

(EL-OH-HEEM tZAH-BAH-OATH) which means God of Hosts Ruling the Universe in Wisdom and Harmony. This aspect of God oversees the scientific and knowledge evolution of the world.

The Archangel that we meet at this level of consciousness is Michael. He is the Prince of Splendor and Wisdom and the Great Protector. Legend has it that the Cherubim were formed from the tears Michael shed over the sins of the faithful. He is the spirit of the planet Mercury and he brings to us the gift of patience. It is very appropriate that he operate in this sphere. Many times, striving for greater and high knowledge can put us in psychic danger, and at those times it is good to have him by our sides.

Working with Michael are the Beni Elohim or the Sons of God. Touching this level presents us with the opportunity to meet and touch with them as well. They are concerned with the transmitting of divine consciousness into the minds of men through greater knowledge. The drive within the individual to "know God" is a result of contact with them.

In this level we awaken the virtue of truth. If there is falsehood in others or deception, or if there is falsehood or deception in ourselves, it can be revealed through contact with this level of consciousness. It is also quite easy, as we grow in our knowledge, to use that knowledge dishonestly. Because of this, the vice that may need to be dealt with and balanced through this level is that of dishonesty. By working with the most positive energies available to us at this level we increase the truth available to us to a degree that dishonesty is unnecessary. We find that the knowledge opens up greater manifestation of that knowledge in our lives—whether through greater health or learning or prosperity. It is this sphere which reveals how.

NETZACH

It is in this emerald-green level of consciousness that we can manifest what is called the "Vision of Beauty Triumphant." This is the kind of beauty that not only leaves us awestruck and speechless, but it lets us know that there must have been a divine hand in its creation. It is the same type of feeling we encounter through inspiring scenes of nature and in those situations which catch and hold our hearts in our throats.

This is, in fact, the level of our emotions and the level where we can begin to really work on areas that touch the heart of us. In astrology, it is linked to the planet Venus. This is the level where we can come to understand more deeply the meaning in relationships, love and the arts. This is the sphere where nature and the love of nature can be unveiled. It is a sphere where we can begin to learn about some of the life forms that exist around us and which we often ignore. We can contact the fairy kingdoms within this sphere, but caution is necessary. This is the level of the emotions, and those of the "fairy" kingdoms work with emotions and can activate them in us in ways that are not beneficial. It is not that they may be trying to do us ill, only that we cannot handle their energies. It creates a condition that is known as being "fairy charmed." We lose our perspective.

Working in this level strengthens our inspiration

and creativity. It can awaken the virtue of unselfishness. An imbalanced awakening and use of the energies at this level can manifest as impurity and lust, and not only on a physical, sexual level. We must remember that Venus is the Goddess of Love, and while in the physical, it is easy for man to misinterpret feelings and direct them in the wrong or least positive manner. This is a level of energy and consciousness that we all must deal with at some time or another. For many this may be difficult, for the Earth is a physical and emotional planet. We are currently living in an emotional age: the Piscean Age. Granted, we are transitioning into the Aquarian Age, a time of raising the emotions to a more spiritual level, but this transition period will activate and increase emotional responses. Thus, it is even more important to take care in working at this level. Remember that the virture we can awaken is unselfishness. This, in essence, is a higher form of emotion, an expression of unconditional love.

The aspect of God that we find operating at this level most strongly is Jehovah Tzabaoth or the God of Hosts. This is appropriate in that we can encounter a host of emotions to be dealt with and thus we would need a God of Hosts in order to bring victory over the emotions. Victory over them is not just conquering them or burying them, but recognizing, utilizing, and expressing the emotions in the most positive and beneficial manner.

Haniel is the Archangel that we meet at this level. She is the Archangel of Love and Harmony and is considered the patron of the arts. Those working in creative fields could do no better than to ask her assistance.

Under Haniel work the Elohim whose name translates into God/Goddesses. They are the actual energies which caused man to translate them as the various deities that make up mythology and religions. They are, in fact, the protectors of religion, and they watch over the leaders of people and help inspire right decisions.

TIPHARETH

This is the level of Beauty, and the gleaming, golden Sun within each of us can be found here. It is the Christ center. It is that place to which we are working in our evolvement: the ability to manifest the Christ consciousness. This is the center of the map, and thus it is through this level that we can harmonize all manifestations of energy. Healing, higher teachers, abundance and success come through this level. It is here that we can touch the Christ center within ourselves.

This awakens a devotion to the Great Work, and we can experience a vision of the harmony of things and an understanding of the mystery of sacrifice. In other words, through this level we can begin to glimpse the universe unfolding as it should. It is here that we truly realize and experience a devotion to working deliberately for the evolution of our soul.

It is the awakening of this center within our planet that has manifested the prevalence of the rainbow, for it is through this center that we unveil the energy and healing abilities, hidden within the rainbow.

It is through this level that we can begin to see the

beauty that lies within all others, regardless of how rough and unpleasing to the eye that the outside might be. Through this level, we see the beauty that lies dormant within ourselves and within others, just as the beauty that lies within the heart of an unopened rose. As we utilize this center, we will find that others will be guided to us. This level connects and touches all levels because there is beauty in all things. This center can give us victory over adversity and make our darker hours clear to our inner sight. It is here that resides the divine child within each of us.

If the energy awakened through this level is unbalanced, it will manifest false pride within us. There are many gifts available to us through this center, but they exist for ALL, *without exception*. Care must be taken not to become smug or overly prideful of those that you do manifest. We must keep in mind that the more we manifest, the more responsible and humble we need to be. They don't make us any better than anyone else or even indicate that we are progressing and evolving more rapidly than others. We each are following our own maps in the manner best suited to ourselves. If we manifest a gift that another has not, it quite simply means that the other person may not have a need to manifest it. There are many paths. None is better than another, and no one can decide what is the best but the person on it.

The aspect of God most strongly active at this level is Jehovah Aloah va Daath or the God of Knowledge and Wisdom. In essence, it is that aspect of God made manifest in the sphere of the mind—realizing tha God operates through our mind if we allow Him.

It is that aspect which rules over the Light of the Universe which relates to the Sun and to the divine Light within each of us, waiting to be unveiled.

Raphael is the Archangel who operates at this level. He is the Angel of Brightness, Beauty, Healing and Life. He is often called the Healer of God, and he will work with us for the directing and ministering of any kind of healing energy. Working with him are the Malachim. They are sometimes referred to as the Virtues or the Angelic Kings. They are the chief bestowers of grace and valor upon mankind. Their principal duty is to work the miracles upon the Earth and in our life. They color our lives with wonder when we touch them.

GEBURAH

Geburah is the level of Severity, Might and Strength. Its temple is bathed in reds, and it is often attributed to the planet Mars. It is here that we can unfold greater energy and courage. We can touch this level for greater initiative, haste and judgment. This level also governs change; the overturning or tearing down of the old to make room for the new.

Working with this level of consciousness will manifest a Vision of Power, an awe of all natural forces and an understanding of their use. It is here that we can realize the power we are capable of controlling, along with a realization of the results of such power and the responsibility necessary for its use. If unbalanced, this level can awaken and manifest cruelty and destruction.

In our society, power is the most sought-after gift and yet is the most abused as well. It can take the form of being cold and unfeeling, as with those who take and give nothing in return. It is this love of power that will conquer those who profess it so strongly. It can take many forms. It may be expressed as the power in royalty, commerce, business, or of war and blood. It burdens those who hold it and control it, and it is ironic that those who are most capable and most fit to bear power are often the ones who put it away from themselves. When we begin to accept the burden of power (which is why we work at this level), we have to learn to contain it as a channel for higher authority. By doing so we make of ourselves a spear of Light, capable of manifesting power on any level in any situation and with any person, but doing so *only* when it is for the good of *all* and according to the free will of all.

The God-Force most active at this level and that manifests most strongly here is Elohim Gibor. This means the God Almighty or the God of Battles, Judging and Avenging Evil and at Whose Steps are Lightning and Flame. It is that aspect of God which cuts away with power what is no longer useful, that the new may come forth.

Kamael is the Archangel that we may meet at this level. He is called the Prince of Strength and Courage. He defends the wronged and will protect the weak. He is the one to work with and call upon when there is a dragon of any form to be slain within our lives. Working with him are the Seraphim, also called the Flaming Ones. They are sometimes called the Powers and working with them will assist us in stopping the efforts of those who would overthrow and upset our world and our individual lives.

CHESED

Chesed is the level we can utilize for greater abundance, growth, organization and prosperity. It is through this sphere that we truly hear the call to the heights. Its temple is the blue temple of Mercy and Justice, and it is often linked to the planet Jupiter. Working in this level of consciousness will help bestow peace and mercy within our lives and will manifest the Vision of Love and True Power on their highest spiritual levels. This is a love without judgment, without assessment, and with no conditions attached to it. It is through this level that we begin to understand the true power of love.

This sphere will awaken the virtue of obedience, but obedience to a higher Will. We learn as we evolve that there is no dishonor in obedience when the command is just. It is only willfulness that receives no recognition or rewards. It is here that we learn the lessons of obedience to our inner self which creates in our lives new freedom and new power over the circumstances of it. We learn that obedience has its place in both the physical and the spiritual realms, but we also learn here that at some point in our evolvement the spiritual must be obeyed at the cost of the physical. This is not such a great sacrifice, for by the time this occurs we have learned the reality of a greater love, a love more spiritual than physical.

If unbalanced, the energies at this level may see us manifesting bigotry and hypocrisy. Both result from a selfish kind of love rather than the more universal expression that is capable of being manifested by contact and work upon this level. This is the level of justice and if there is to be such, then we must look beyond the surface and the superficial and give obedience to higher principles.

The God-Force most active at this level is El or God, the Mighty One. He rules with glory, magnificence and grace, and the realization of that is touched when we begin to touch this level.

Tzadkiel is the Archangel whom we meet at this temple. He is called the Prince of Mercy and Beneficence. He was the protecting Angel of Abraham and is often called the Guard to the Gate of the East Winds. He directs the work of the Chasmalim at this level. They are an Order of Angels called the Brilliant Ones and they are sometimes referred to as the Dominations. It is through them that the majesty of God is manifested through all worlds and in all men. It is through them that we can realize the majesty of ourselves in communion with the majesty of God.

BINAH

Binah is the sphere wherein lies Understanding. It can be linked to Saturn-like influences astrologically. Saturn is the teacher who teaches us that through patience and time we can come to understand that which has been hidden from us. For this reason, this sphere can be visualized as black because all colors are hidden within black. The black veils the divine glory until time and understanding reveal it. This is the level at which to find the understanding of situations that have been difficult and obscure to us. The God-Force operating is Jehovah Elohim. This is that aspect of God which manifests the perfection of creation and the life of the world to come. This sphere enables us to understand the perfect process of life and all the situations we encounter within it.

Tzaphkiel is the Archangel. He is the Prince of Spiritual Strife against Evil. Through his assistance at this level we can understand those things which confront us in life and learn how to overcome them in the most effective, spiritual manner. He is also the keeper of the akashic records which can be revealed to us with time and effort to increase our understanding. He is also very appropriate for this sphere in that any strife in our life (especially spiritual) is an indication of a need for greater understanding. Entering into his level and calling upon him will bring us that understanding.

The Aralim are the Angels working under him. They are called the Strong and Mighty Ones which is also appropriate because they are often needed to help sustain us long enough through strife to achieve the understanding. They are sometimes called the Thrones. They are appointed over the grass, trees, fruit, grain—in essence, all of Mother Earth. They can help us to understand the intimate relationship we have with all of Mother Earth and help us to understand that everything we do to Mother Earth will ultimately affect us as well. And all we need to do is enter into this level and call upon them for assistance.

The virtue awakened in this sphere is that of silence. This is also appropriate in that silence is necessary in order to hear, and through hearing comes understanding. If unbalanced, the energy at this level may manifest as avarice—clutching everything and everyone to us rather than understanding that nothing is separate from us.

This level of consciousness helps us to understand that understanding comes from seeing what we must struggle through and give out in order to grow. It is here that we learn how restriction and forms and limitations operate within our lives. It is here that we can touch and understand the mysteries of birth and death.

CHOKMAH

Chokmah is the level and world of Wisdom in its truest form. Its world can be visualized as a cloud-like gray, a transparent, pearl-hued mist. It contains the divine light found in Kether, but now it is mixed with all the other colors, radiating its grayish tones. The God-Force within it is Yah, meaning Divine, Ideal Wisdom. Within its realms are all the starry heavens, so when we touch it, we can also touch the stars!

The Archangel is Ratziel, the Prince of the Knowledge of Hidden and Concealed Things (those things hidden behind the cloud of gray). He works within this level to help us to come to a greater wisdom of how the universe operates. He helps us to see the wisdom behind its operation on all levels. The Order of

Angels under his guidance is the Auphanim or Whirling Forces. It is through them that come the spiritual experience that we ultimately seek at this level—a vision of God face to face.

In essence this is seeing the divine wisdom "at work" within the universe. The experience is a vision and we must remember that a vision is not the same as seeing the actual thing, but it is powerful enough to instill a devotion beyond any piety experienced before. This sphere of consciousness awakens us to the devotion and pure wonder at the wisdom that has lay hidden within us all the while—a wisdom that transcends simple revelations and extraordinary perceptions.

This level can be considered a pure source of energy; life-giving energy. It is here that things are put in motion. It is here that we can learn how to put things in motion in their purest essence.

KETHER

Kether is the Crown. It is the deepest level. It was the first manifestation out of that limitless energy of the Divine. Through it would come all the other sephiroth. It is not any more spiritual than any of the other sephiroth or levels of consciousness. It was simply the first one that came forth from the Nothingness and is the one that is closest to it. It is a level of consciousness of pure Light—a divine white brilliance. It is the last level we touch and awaken to its fullest before reuniting again with God.

The God-Force of Kether is Eheieh (EH-HEH-YEH). This was the name given to Moses from out of the burning bush, the "I Am that I Am." At this level of consciousness, the force of God is simply there and cannot truly be comprehended by man because it is so close to that from which it came. It simply is. At this level, there is the growing realization that God is an ever-present fact—always was and always shall be a divine companion for all of creation.

The Archangel is Metatron who is considered the greatest of the angelic beings. His task is to sustain mankind, and it is he that gave to man the Qabala so that we may regain our true destiny. Under him is an Order of Angels called the Chaioth ha-Qadesh, the Holy Living Creatures. They are the Angels of Love, Light and Fire in its most spiritual aspects. They are sometimes referred to as the Seraphim. They can help us to understand the Qabala and our own evolutionary process.

At this level, there is no vice. There is only the virtue of completing the Great Work. Once we do that, we re-enter that Nothingness. Because the force in this sephira, as in the next two as well, is so strong, they can only be experienced in their purest form when all the other levels have been awakened and balanced and comprehended. Meditation and reflection upon them and their aspects though will lead to greater understanding of the power at those levels which came after. Working at this level will open new ideas and conceptions, ones that reach far into the future. It opens doors to "pure" research and the unusual, the surprising and beyond. It opens us to thoughts that have not been considered yet. It is here that we can begin to see the beginning of all things and

also the final ending of all things. It is here that we can
touch the Creator—the Alpha and the Omega.

It is true that we live in a physical world—but not
entirely. Just as we can sit in our homes and allow our
minds to take us back to the events of the past where
we can relive emotions and ideas, so can the Qabala
take us back to other realms. Through it, through the
sephiroth, we are able to touch these other realms and
awaken the innate abilities and potentials that exist
within us in those realms. We can then bring them
back and apply them to the physical one in which we
are primarily focused.

These sephiroth are not states of consciousness
wherein we can escape life and avoid situations, but
rather they should be utilized to enable us to seek out
life more directly for the lessons and gifts and growths
that it can bring.

We have the map. We now know some of the
terrain. What follows are the means to enter the terrain. Just as we can use a car, bus, plane or train to
travel in the physical, we also have various modes of
travel to the more ethereal and spiritual realms on
which we can operate. They are available to all and
they are easy to reach. But if we want to walk on water,
we have to get out of the boat!

Chapter 5

The Power of Sound, Symbolism and Invocation

In the spheres a wonderful harmony of sound is being produced eternally, and from that source have all things been created.
—Florence Crane

For by names and images are all Powers awakened and reawakened.
—Occult Principle

In a society that is highly technological and often much more complicated than we would like, we tend to assume that the mysterious and the mystical must be even more so. Unfortunately, this is a misconception that many have. When they encounter the Qabala in their metaphysical studies, this misconception is reinforced. It is true that there are many facets and intricacies to the Qabala, but it is not true that we must have knowledge of all these intricacies to work in a positive and productive manner with it. As in all things, when overwhelmed, it is time to simplify.

The Qabala, no matter at what level we work with it, is based upon some very basic universal laws and principles. These principles and laws operate through all areas of metaphysics and spirituality. They are *universal*. They are *not* strictly Qabalistic. It does not matter whether one is a beginner on the path to self-evolvement or a fourth degree initiate. The principles and laws with which you must work to progress on your path are the same. These laws and principles permeate every system of development. Understanding them and working with them is what opens to you your greatest potentials and capabilities.

They are principles that the beginner as well as the initiate use to more effectually take control of their lives and the circumstances of their growth. In fact, the only difference between the initiate and the beginner is that the initiate is already familiar with these principles and uses them consistently while the beginner does not. It is these principles which open the doors to all the levels of consciousness found within the Qabalistic system of development.

The Principle of Energy

We live in a world of energy. Everything in our world is energy in one form or another. All matter—animal, vegetable and mineral—is energy. Nothing is truly solid. Every substance is composed of minute particles called atoms. Atoms are the building blocks of physical matter, and they are composed of protons, neutrons and electrons. These are not actually particles themselves, but as science has discovered are actually subtle vibrations that appear to be attuned to a more cosmic force within the universe. Atoms that have similar vibrational patterns combine to form the various physical manifestations about us, whether it be a stone, plant or human organ. With a powerful enough microscope, one can detect that that which was thought solid is not really solid at all. The atoms that comprise it are in motion; the electrons and protons are moving constantly. The density at which they combine determines the type of matter. Thus, rock has a greater density of atoms within it than water. Both contain atoms, but the water atoms are more loosely combined. Neither is truly solid.

The ancients were very much aware of this. They may not have used the same terminology, but they knew that everything was energy. They knew everything had a vibratory rate. They knew that energy particles combined to form matter, but they also knew that outside of matter itself there existed an infinite supply of energy that had not combined to form matter. They knew that this energy surrounded and permeated man on all levels. It was and still is a virtually untapped source of energy supply.

The ancients called this energy *fohat*. This energy, which constitutes our atmosphere and our universe, is electomagnetic in property. It simply flows free, as if waiting to be drawn upon by man. There have been those in the past who did draw upon it and utilized it to their fullest. And it is from the lives of these people that come the stories of miracles and wonders and magic. We tend to believe today that such things as "miracles" are for only the select few, the gifted. Nothing could be further from the truth. It is for *all—without exception*!

Every person has the capability of utilizing this universal energy for their benefit, and the methods are neither intricate or complicated. In fact, they are so simple as to be almost unbelievable. Utilizing these methods in conjunction with an organized system of evolvement, such as the Qabala, does more than expand awareness and reveal potentials. It reveals to each of us in its own way just how closely connected we are to each other and to the Divine. It places us in a position of being responsible for all that makes up our lives. It demonstrates that we are in control. We have the capability of acting rather than being acted upon. It demonstrates that we are not at the mercy of our circumstances. We do not have to suffer. Suffering is only good for the soul if it teaches us how not to suffer. We have the capability to enjoy life to its fullest and extract from it all the knowledge we can. Then from these towers of knowledge we can build bridges of wisdom which link them together and draw us closer to our divine origin. And it all begins by learning to utilize the universal energy to which we all have access.

As stated, this energy is "free floating." It is simply neutral. Until it is focused it does not become a force that we can utilize. This the ancients knew, and it was the focusing of this energy that constituted much of the learning in the ancient Mystery Schools. There are many ways of focusing energy and thus creating a force: visualization, light, sound, color, meditation, etc. The focusing pulls the surrounding energy together. The projection of thought, sound or color, for example, draws the free floating energy atoms together, concentrating them into a force. This force can then be utilized for whatever purpose we desire. Remember that energy is *neutral*. It is only the manner in which it is utilized that determines its quality.

The Principle of Thought

All energy follows thought. This is a universal axiom of energy. This means that energy is focused and becomes a force through the direction of our thoughts (our brain wave concentration). This is why all the Masters urged discipline of the mind, control of the thoughts. They knew that it focused and moved energy. We live in an energy field that surrounds us and penetrates us on all levels. Focus and concentration of thought enables us to direct and apply this energy for whatever means we desire. The greater the concentration, the greater and quicker the effect. This universal energy is neutral and impersonal. It exists and operates for everyone *without exception*. It is neither negative or positive in itself; that is determined by its use, but it does operate in a very literal manner according to our thoughts.

Thoughts shape our current world, our own individual experiences. Every thought we think is responded to whether by our own inner being or the outer world around us. Even though they are mental, they affect the physical plane. In ancient Kahuna teachings, man is considered to have three selves: high, middle and low. The low self is that part of our subconscious that maintains our physical body and looks for commands, wishes and desires to bring into reality. It is through its abilities that things manifest in our physical life. It has an elemental consciousness—a literal consciousness. It doesn't reason or make choices. It simply experiences everything literally, including all of our thoughts and feelings. The low self builds a self-image and the physical world by all that is received by it from our conscious, everyday state of mind. Thus, everything we say or think about ourselves will be put into manifestation by that aspect of our subconscious.

How often do people (including ourselves) think or say, "That was so stupid of me!" 'I don't have any talent." "That's unbelievable." "That's impossible." "Things always seem to go wrong." And then we wonder why our lives are such a mess.

Thoughts shape our world because they mold the energy surrounding us into manifestation. It puts that energy in motion. How we concentrate and focus our thoughts determines what we will or will not experience. Our thoughts become self-fulfilling prophecies. If our thoughts lean toward the negative, we see the negative manifest within our lives. If they lean toward the positive, we manifest positive conditions.

Thought is the process of creating images, and it is these images that focus and direct the universal energy around us. The image speaks to the subconscious which begins to focus the energies accordingly, whether it be to unlock latent abilities or manifest greater prosperity.

Change the imaginings and we change the world. In other words, by taking control of our thoughts and the images created by them and directing them to particular levels and planes, we open the doors to all the levels of our subconscious and all the wonders of the world. By working with the Qabala and learning to focus our thoughts and images upon the aspects associated with it, we manifest a higher consciousness and a world of unlimited possibilities.

Part of the process of evolvement is learning to look beyond our immediate senses, to expand our awareness and our consciousness, to recognize energy and activity, even when not visible to the naked eye. We are trying to raise ourselves above the physical by taking greater control of it. This means we need to recognize life and motion on levels not readily seen. There is more to our world than can be recognized by the five senses and our conscious mind. Our growth entails realizing this at some point. We have to work beyond the conscious minded manner of living, to open ourselves to other realities, to our unlimited unconscious and thereby break down the limitations of life that we have imposed upon ourselves.

This is why visualization and symbolism are not only essential to working with the Qabala but are essential to expanding our consciousness. Visualization is a focusing of our thoughts. The longer we can hold the visual image and the greater the intensity we can evoke from it, the greater the power of the thoughts, the quicker the manifestation.

Much of the Qabala is symbolic. Working with it involves focusing our thoughts upon images, visualizations and symbols. It is the focusing upon these that triggers the response within our subconscious, for the images have a vibrational rate that corresponds to various levels of our subconscious.

This triggering aspect is called resonance. Resonance is a quality of vibration. In essence, energy is intoned or projected (whether through thought, images, sound, etc.). It then seeks out that which is of a similar vibration. In an earlier chapter we discussed how all the energies and vibrations of the universe also exist within us at some level. (Malkuth is the recipient of all the energies.) This projection of energy seeks out those similar vibrations within us, creating a response. This process is called a sympathetic vibration. This response awakens a particular level of our being and stimulates it into activity. By knowing which level of our being that we wish to stimulate, we can then use the images, symbols and thoughts associated with that level to initiate the process.

It is not as complicated as what it might seem upon the surface. Our conscious mind is normally so cluttered with everyday aspects of living that it takes a stronger focus of energy to stimulate us or take us beyond the conscious level of life to other levels. We use the images and symbols and colors and sounds to assist this process. These methods of focusing energy allow us to tap an unlimited reserve of energy and ability at levels that we have allowed to remain untouched.

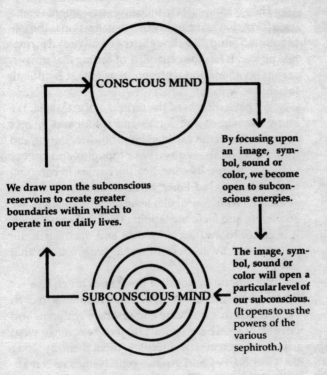

CONSCIOUS MIND

By focusing upon an image, symbol, sound or color, we become open to subconscious energies.

We draw upon the subconscious reservoirs to create greater boundaries within which to operate in our daily lives.

The image, symbol, sound or color will open a particular level of our subconscious. (It opens to us the powers of the various sephiroth.)

SUBCONSCIOUS MIND

Drawing Upon the Subconscious

The Principle of Sound

The greatest asset in focusing our thoughts creating a force that can amplify the visualization is the use of sound. Sound, like thought, is a creative and formative power. It has the capability of setting that universal energy in motion with an intensity that is difficult to achieve without.

We have discussed the terrain of the Qabala. We know the names and forces and colors and images associated with the various sephiroth. Meditating and thinking upon them directs our thoughts and energy to those spheres. By sounding the names, in conjunction with the God-Force or angelic image or color associated with a particular level of consciousness, we accelerate and facilitate tapping the level's resources. It is easier to awaken, stimulate and draw forth the powers and awareness inherent within us at that level.

We vibrate or vocalize the names much like we would any mantram. We give equal emphasis to each syllable, hearing it vibrate and resonate within us and outside of us. These sounds help us to achieve what may have been greatly difficult without them. By using the God Names and Archangelic Names as a mantram, the sound of the name seeks out that power. It resonates to the hibernating force deep within us. If we couple the sound with a visualization or image, we accelerate the awakening within us of the power and energy and potential to which we are heirs.*

---

* Ancient occult knowledge teaches that, depending upon tone and volume, the human voice has the power of molding the substance of astral light into various shapes and forms; thus its creative ability.

As stated earlier, all things (including sound) are forms of energy and differ only in the rate of vibration. This includes both the visible and invisible realms of life. In order for things to adhere together, they must vibrate together. To change the vibration will either destroy the form or bring about mutations or alterations.

Everyone has seen examples of how glass can be shattered with the correct high pitched tone. This is an altering of the vibration basic to the form of the glass. Things do not have to be destroyed, however. Changing the vibration in the proper manner can alter the form, and it can be done in creative ways. We use sound as a mantram, as a focus to alter the vibration of our own energy field, altering it enough to vibrate more in unison with the level of consciousness or force we are attempting to awaken and stimulate within us. Just as ice can become water and even steam by altering the rate of vibration of its molecules, we can also alter our own states of consciousness by changing our own vibrational rates. This is enhanced through the use of sound.

All life is in motion. Every atom of every molecule of every cell in every person, animal, plant, thought, emotion—everything seen or unseen—vibrates because all life (animate and inanimate) is *energy*.

Vibration is most easily detected on physical levels. This can be observed easily simply by monitoring our own metabolism as we age. This is what is known as the transmutation of energies, altering its form and vibrational pattern for new and varied purposes.

We must keep in mind that we are much more

than just physical life. Our consciousness touches more than just our physical vehicle. We are also composed of bands of energy reflecting our emotional, mental and spiritual states as well. These bands of energy are often referred to as our subtle bodies, and they are intimately connected to our physical vehicle and to the essence which constitute the true *self*. These subtle bodies also have vibrational patterns. By learning to work with the energy vibrations of all our subtle bodies and levels of consciousness that touch them, we can begin to open ourselves to that Divine Spark, those higher potentialities, residing in the various levels of our consciousness. We can learn to transmute the negative energies that hinder and limit our growth and evolvement, and vibrate an energy that resonates with the fulfillment, abundance, health, prosperity and love that we need and desire.

The most dynamic method of altering and transmuting energies and conditions (physical and spiritual) is through the use of sounds and tones. In all of the world's cosmologies, sound has always been considered the basis of existence. Through sound (and its vibration) man/woman and this world came into being and continue to be sustained. Sacred sound—whether as music, songs, incantations, or chants—is a vital force which permeates all aspects of creation. In the Christian religion, the book of John states, "In the beginning was the word and the word was with God and the word was God . . ." According to the Qabalistic traditions, the world came into existence through the utterance of the sacred name of God, the Tetragrammaton YVHV. In Egypt, Thoth used words in order to create the universe, calling out over the waters. And so it goes throughout the world.

Sound has always been considered a direct link between humanity and the gods. At some point, all of the ancient Mystery Schools taught their disciples and students the use of sound as a creative and healing force, whether through the use of music or voice. Sound has always been considered the oldest method of altering vibration to instill healing energies. It was used in the Mystery Schools of Greece, China, India, and among the American Indians. The Essenes, a branch of the Great White Brotherhood who were the overseers of the early training and education of the Master we call Jesus, were highly practiced in the use of sound. They were called the "soft-spoken ones" because of their ability to use vocal tones and sounds as an alchemical and healing force.

Regardless of the cosmology, they all had several things in common with their teachings. Sound and chanting could effect healing within a person, as could rhythmic movements (either in dance or stomping). They taught that rhythm could effect changes in the physical state of an individual and that melody would affect the emotions, while harmony was capable of lifting the consciousness to spiritual awareness. Chants, mantras and prayers served the purpose of re-achieving the union between body, mind and soul, and thus expanding awareness and consciousness.

We must remember that sound is a major contributing factor to our present state of consciousness. The difference between the random sounds of daily life and what is called "directed esoteric sound" is that the latter produces greater harmony within our being rather than dissonance. Esoteric sound, and its uses within the Qabala, is a *major* factor in achieving higher states of consciousness.

The human voice can produce two aspects of sounds: vowels and consonants. Vowel sounds within the various Names of Power associated with the Qabala are for creating harmony and for bringing the energies outside of us into a focus to where they can then act within us on other levels of our consciousness. Consonants within the various Names and Words of Power of the Qabala serve more for inner awareness and development. When combined, as in the God Names associated with the various levels, we integrate inner and outer awareness, increasing our energies and opening higher potentialities.

The human voice is our primary creative and musical instrument. It has the power to connect inner and outer worlds. It has the power to also integrate them within our own individual energy fields. It is an expression for our emotional and spiritual natures.

Voice releases *power*! It releases it in the direction of our thoughts, thereby sending energy to those areas of our consciousness or physical body. Because every cell of our being is a sound resonator, we can enhance the effects by using the voice musically to intone the various Names. In the following chart, certain musical notes have been assigned to the various levels of the Tree of Life. Intoning the God Names or Angelic Names in that particular tone enhances and releases even greater energy to that level of our consciousness. The designations are ones that work well for me because of the symbolism and effects upon physical energy in relation to these tones. Because I have built a symbolic thought-form around these particular designations, they work best for me. As you work to explore and grow, you may find that other tones seem to resonate better with you in association to the various sephiroth. That is legitimate. Remember that it is our responsibility to use the information and the Tree of Life in the manner that is best for you. Yes, there are guidelines, but you also must be able to adapt it to yourself.

Singing the names has tremendous power. Singing links us with the underlying substance of *all* things and *all* beings. It can react esoterically upon the universe itself. It is a means of entering into a relationship with the most occult powers. It is the most creative act of the voice. Words have power, but when words are placed within a musical tone or melody, that power becomes *universal*.

Many enter into the study of the Qabala to learn "secret and powerful" names—looking for the quick and easy way to development. It is said that to know someone's name is to have power over them. There is much truth *and* much misconception in that. Unless we know the metaphysics and all the significant correlations of every sound within a name, we cannot have power over it.

Yes, words—especially the Names associated with the Qabala—do have their own "magic" if we know how to use them. These ancient Names associated with the Qabala affect moderns differently than in the past because we live in an entirely different environ-

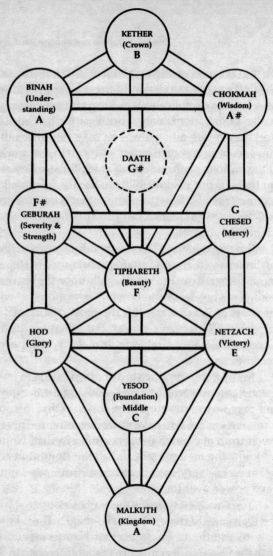

MUSIC OF THE SPHERES—Linking musical tones to the various sephiroth and intoning the Names of Power in that musical note will amplify the effects and create a stronger link to that level.

ment, but they are still effective if trained in their use. *It is not the words that have been worth keeping secret. The real mystery lies in the practice and usage of the words.*

The God and Archangelic Names of the Qabala are specific call signals linked with the different levels of our consciousness and those beings that can work with us most strongly upon those levels. Because they have been used over and over throughout the ages, they have established a direct connection between divine intelligence and human intelligence.

We use the names to invoke the energies within ourselves. We should be aware of the inner reality that the God Names link us to. These names we vibrate are the keys that admit us to the inner worlds. We intone them in several steps:

1. Set the mouth and throat for making the sound.
2. Take a full, deep breath.
3. Press the air steadily out of the body.
4. Each syllable should receive equal emphasis.
5. When the name can be sustained for around 15 seconds, then we alternate the outsound with an *insound*. An insound is not audible, but is vibrated silently after having vibrated it audibly. Insounds are received on the inner planes.
6. As we exhale, we intone the name audibly. As we inhale, we intone the name silently, making the same exact sound as when audible.

7. The aim is to create a constant sound of
the name varying from one dimension
to the other, thus linking the inner world
to the outer world.

This is when the real alchemical energy change begins
to occur.

The names that we sound or vibrate out loud and
internally are a summary of all the images and forces
and powers associated with them. The thoughts, the
symbols, the colors and the sounds *all* work together.
They can and do work separately to open doors to
other planes of existence and other states of consciousness. They can and do work separately to awaken
and stimulate into activity our higher inherent abilities
and potentials, but *together* they facilitate and accelerate
the process.

We live in a fast society. We encounter changes
every day of such quantity that it boggles the conscious mind, but it is only boggling because we do not
use all of our resources. There is a need to catch up,
and for those wanting a way to move ahead and take
greater control of their lives, the means is available.
Using all of the methods of focusing energy in the
right manner is the simplest and safest way to begin
tapping our unlimited resources. It is the simplest way
to uncover the treasures within our map.

In the chapters ahead, we will examine specific
ways of employing all these to uncover our treasures,
but we must realize that it is not a complicated process. It is simply utilizing very *basic* principles of life
and energy. Unfortunately, it is often hard for many to

simplify on any level, but growing in this age (as in all ages) begins with realizing that there is often as much to unlearn as there is to learn.

We now know the principles and laws upon which "miracles" and fulfillment are based. We now know that we are all energy. We now know how to focus that energy available to tap and utilize our own natural abilities and powers in ways we have yet to imagine. All that remains is the doing. And that is the true magic of life!

Chapter 6

Touching the Powers

> *Sitting in your chair you can travel further than ever Columbus traveled and to Lordlier worlds than his eyes had rested on. Are you not tired of surfaces? Come with me and we will bathe in the fountain of youth. I can point you the way to El Dorado.*
>
> *—Candle of Vision*

As we meditate upon and work with the sephiroth and their various associations, we awaken that level of consciousness which is most closely attuned to it. These levels of consciousness are far more than simple imaginings, they are realities in and of themselves. They are distinct from physical reality as we know it, but they are actual planes of life. It is by using the Tree of Life that we learn to safely touch these other planes and learn of our potential and how to manifest it more positively in our physical environment.

We live primarily within the physical world, but

we operate and are touched by other planes of life as well. How often have we been at work, executing our tasks routinely, and yet our mind is on the events of the previous night or the trip planned for the coming weekend. We operate on many levels other than the physical. By increasing our awareness of them, we can improve the conditions of the main level in which we operate. These levels are just as real as the physical, and they can teach us much more about ourselves and the world in which we live. But we must utilize them first.

We are, in essence, shape-shifters and alchemists in our physical world, whether we realize it or not. We alter our moods, manners, styles, actions and reactions every day to the people and situations around us into whatever style or tone will enable us to "survive." When we refer to touching these other planes, these other levels of our consciousness, we do so to bring forth increased awareness and realization of the divine within us. By doing so we enable this divine aspect of our being to operate more actively and positively in our lives. We are attempting to awaken a more permanent "shape-shift" in our lives—a change that aligns itself more with the Divine will and power that can be a part of our daily lives. This increases the control and focus over our life situations, and we find that we are no longer at the mercy of our life circumstances.

The idea that we must suffer and sacrifice and struggle every inch of the way thorugh our life, especially if we are trying to hasten our evolvement, is a very *wrong* one. Certainly there must be work and there must be effort and discipline, but that does not mean the same as suffering. Suffering is only good for the soul if it teaches us how not to suffer again. The growth process should involve joy and fascination and wonderment. If it does not, then something is wrong and we do not have a true understanding of the life process.

The levels of consciousness, and the planes of existence that we touch through them, are full of wondrous and beautiful things. It has much to fascinate and much to appall. Remember that we work on these levels to break down the limitations we have imposed upon ourselves. The breaking down of the limitations puts us in a position where we have to look at ourselves. We have to bring forth aspects of ourselves that we may have hidden away. As appalling as some of those aspects may be when we bring them forth, they also come with a special gift. They open us to aspects of ourselves that fill us with a wonder and joy and fulfillment that cannot be achieved in other ways. The old is always replaced by the new, and the new will be more beneficial to your future growth and well-being!

These levels of consciousness and planes of existence are not escapes. We don't use them to avoid life, but rather we use them to seek out the lessons of life that will most fulfill us as individuals. We invite the lessons and tests and learnings because they show us the potential we are capable of manifesting in our day-to-day life. By working with them we take responsibility and control over our life and our circumstances. We begin to see the relationships between our own states of consciousness. We begin to see the relationships of all of Nature and life to ourselves. We then begin to integrate this awareness and knowledge on all levels of our life. It is then we see the effects. Things seem to work. Situations take care of themselves. Problems and difficulties are less troublesome. People are more responsive to us. By changing our world and expanding our consciousness, we have altered the world outside of us. We have made it more pleasant, more fruitful and more joyful.

Procedure
Step One: Choosing the Level

The first few times that you touch the various levels of consciousness, it is best to do so starting with Malkuth and then working up to Kether. Keep in mind that most of these are virtually untapped levels of consciousness and power within. Because the ones at the bottom of the Tree of Life are closer to the "normal" consciousness level, they will be easier to tap. That does not mean they aren't as fruitful as the ones higher up on the Tree. It just means that you will have easier access to the lower ones in the beginning. By the time you have touched the lower, you will have acquired some experience and understanding of how it actually operates, and this will make accessing the other levels of consciousness easier.

It must be remembered that each level actually has levels within it, so each time you touch a sephira you can acquire greater and deeper depths of awareness and knowledge. In fact, the levels within each sephira are infinite in themselves. Realize that the first "touching" is the first step to initiating yourself

Sephira	Acquisitions from each Sephira
Kether	Greater creativity; any final ending information; inner spiritual quest and its causes and attainment.
Chokmah	Greater personal initiative; a source of energy which puts things in motion; Father-type information; realization of one's abilities.
Binah	Greater understanding of sorrows and burdens; Mother-type information; understanding on its deepest level; for strength through silence; understanding anything secretive.
Chesed	Greater sense of obedience to higher; financial gains, opportunities; building the new; justice; abundance; prosperity; hearing the inner call.
Geburah	Greater energy and courage; for tearing down of old forms; for change of any kind; critical judgment; information on enemies and discord.
Tiphareth	Greater and higher sense of devotion; all matters of healing, life and success; for harmony on any level and any matter; awakening of Christ consciousness; glory and fame.
Netzach	Greater unselfishness; understanding and energy power in relationships; sexuality and elements of nature; creativity and the arts; love and idealism.
Hod	Greater truthfulness; revealing of falsehood and deception around us; greater ability in communications, learning, magic, wheelings and dealings.
Yesod	Greater sense of true independence and confidence; greater intuition and psychic ability; mental and emotional health; dreamwork; understanding and recognition of the tides of change.
Malkuth	Greater ability to discriminate in your life; to overcome a sense of inertia in life; physical health problems of self and others; affairs of home; greater self-discovery; elemental life.

(This table lists some of the uses for tapping the various levels of consciousness. It is not necessary to limit yourself to them, but rather recognize that it is only to be used as a guideline.)

into the higher and holy mysteries of life.

After you have worked through all of the levels at least once, you should have a good working knowledge of the procedure and methods involved. This familiarity gives you a little more freedom to operate at those levels. You can then choose the level according to the purpose you desire.

The chart on page 83 should serve as a brief reminder as to what can be tapped from the various levels. Do not limit yourself to this. You will find that there are things that you as an individual can acquire from these levels that are not listed. Part of the enjoyment of working with the Qabala is discovering just how much really is available to you at each level. Do not allow this list to limit you. It is only a guideline to follow in the beginning, at best, and it is fractional.

Step Two: Altering the Energy Field

After you have chosen the level at which you wish to work, begin the process of enabling yourself to tap that level. This can be facilitated in a very simple manner. Remember from the previous chapter that universal energy surrounds and permeates us on all levels. Focus this energy in the area in which you will be doing your work to be more conducive to a vibrational rate that will resonate with the sephirotic level of consciousness. By attuning and focusing the energy around you to a frequency that corresponds to the energy you are going to tap within, it becomes much easier to not only reach the level of consciousness but to tap into it as well.

Candles and incense are two of the easiest and

most effective means of creating an energy field around you conducive to the level of consciousness you are seeking to touch. Light candles in the environment that are of the same color as what is associated with the level of consciousness (the sephira). The color of the candle has a vibrational rate that will resonate with the level of consciousness in which you are working. By lighting the candle within the environment you put the energy of its color into the atmosphere around you. Thus the energy in the area is not only more conducive to the level of consciousness you are attempting, but it also creates resonance within you—assisting you in achieving that level more quickly.

Certain incenses, perfumes and oils also focus energy in the same manner as color. There are certain fragrances that have a vibrational rate that also assist in stimulating those levels of consciousness you are trying to touch. By using the fragrance in conjunction with the candles you alter the energy around you and begin the process of stimulating the corresponding levels of consciousness within you. In fact, because of their vibrational patterns, they open the pathways to other levels of consciousness. Vibrational stimulation such as with color, fragrance or sound, assists you in moving past the conscious mind to the subconscious. It attunes the energy field of your environment and thus of your own self to more closely align to the level you wish to touch.

Unlike the colors, the incenses associated with various levels of consciousness or sephiroth are often arbitrary. The ones listed are to be used only as a guideline. As you continue your studies and grow in

Sephira	Color of Candle	Fragrance
Kether	White	Frankincense, Ambergris
Chokmah	Gray	Eucalyptus, Musk, Geranium
Binah	Black	Myrrh, Chamomile
Chesed	Blue	Bayberry, Cedar, Nutmeg
Geburah	Red	Cypress, Pine, Tobacco, Gardenia
Tiphareth	Yellow	Rose, Jasmine
Netzach	Green	Rose, Patchouli, Bayberry
Hod	Orange	Rosemary, Frangipani, Wisteria
Yesod	Violet	Lavender, Myrtle, Honeysuckle
Malkuth	Citrine, Olive, Russet or Black	Sandalwood, Lemon, Carnation

your awareness, you will realize that any fragrance will help induce an altered state of consciousness. Some practice and trial of various fragrances will help each individual to decide which is best for him/her. If unsure, an ordinary church incense or frankincense will suffice.* A study of aromatherapy will assist in determining what will work best for you.

---

* Frankincense is a fragrance which has a strong, cleansing vibration to it. It cleanses the human aura and its environment of negativity, purifying the area. This allows for easier altering of the consciousness.

Step Three: Achieving the Altered State

Step two will have set the energy in the environment and have begun the process of stimulating the level of consciousness you are going to touch. Although an important aspect, it alone will not complete the process for you. You still have to allow yourself to relax enough to permit step two to unlock the doors for you.

Relaxation is the key! There are many methods of relaxing. Experimentation will let you know which one or combination of methods works best for you. A seated position is best simply because most people are programmed to think that when they lie down, they sleep. You do not want to sleep; just relax.

Essentially, what you are attempting to do is alter your brain wave pattern. In a normal, waking state of consciousness, your brain puts out what are called *beta* waves. As you relax, the brainwave pattern alters, and it emits what are called *alpha* waves. There are varying degrees of alpha states (states of relaxation), but you do not have to achieve a deep alpha state of consciousness to gain results or tap the levels. In the beginning just achieving an altered state of consciousness will do. As you practice and work, you will find it easier to achieve deeper states that will open new levels within the sephiroth for you. This takes time, patience, practice and persistence.

Developing the art of relaxation and meditation is necessary for evolvement. It gives control. It helps to build energy and to begin to discriminate between what are your thoughts and what is being impressed upon you from another level of consciousness or even outside of you. There are many forms of meditation and relaxation. That is because there are so many individuals within the world. You do not have to limit yourself to one. Try several methods and then extract what you can from it to develop the method that is best for you as an individual.

In the beginning the use of progressive relaxation is a very effective method to utilize. The procedure is simple. Place yourself in a seated position and make yourself comfortable. *Make sure you are not and cannot be disturbed.* This means taking the phone off the hook and informing others in the house to respect your quiet time. The reason for this is very simple. When in an altered state of consciousness, you develop what is termed "hyperaesthesia." You become highly sensitive. Therefore, a phone ringing will be intensified to the point where it can be painful. Certainly, there are some sounds that you can do nothing about. For those, you should close them out as best you can, but most extraneous noise can be controlled.

The next step in the progressive relaxation process is that of visualizing and imagining each part of your body from the feet to the head as being filled with warmth, comfort and relaxation. Remember that energy follows thought, so as you think and visualize this, the energy within you and around you will respond to warm, comfort and relax that particular part of the body. Take your time with this procedure. The more relaxed you become, the easier it is to tap the various levels of consciousness within your being and the deeper you can tap into them.

The more you work at this, the easier it will

become. In essence, you are training your conscious mind to relax and allow the subconscious to be released in a controlled manner. With persistence and practice, you will find that it becomes easier. You will discover that it won't be necessary to spend 15 or 20 minutes just on the relaxation process. You will discover that by setting the atmosphere with candles and fragrances and sitting in preparation to tap these levels will in themselves be all that is necessary to achieve the relaxation. Thus the time involved is less and thus you have greater opportunity to extract even greater amounts from your other levels of being.

In the beginning, you may find yourself encountering what has been termed "resistance." Resistance only occurs at the subconscious level. You may find your mind wandering or arguing with you over what you are attempting. *This is a positive sign!* This is a signal that you have tapped your subconscious mind. You may even encounter levels of resistance; these are nothing more than the depths and limitations that you have allowed to prevent you from tapping your own innate abilities and potentials.

When the mind wanders, do not get upset. Becoming upset only serves to bring you back to a conscious level state of mind. Mind wandering is a form of resistance too. The mind is wandering because the subconscious mind is used to being in control and is not used to being directed. When this occurs, simply bring your attention back to your point of focus. You may have to do this a number of times in the beginning. It is simply a part of the learning process. You are training the subconscious mind to follow your directions more closely. You are training yourself to be in greater control of your consciousness. By simply bringing the attention back to its point of focus, you reinforce the subconscious mind that it is under your control. You are developing higher discipline.

> *Remember:*
> 1. Find a comfortable place.
> 2. A seated position is better.
> 3. Close your eyes to eliminate visual distractions.
> 4. Remove the phone and eliminate any auditory distractions.
> 5. Take your time with the progressive relaxation. The more relaxed you are, the greater the access to your subconscious mind.

Step Four: Tapping Your Inner Realms

The first three steps simply set the stage. This is the crucial step. It is the step in which you enter the various levels. It is at this point that you will begin to use those principles of energy that were discussed earlier.

As you sit relaxed with eyes closed, begin to visualize the color associated with the level at which you are going to work. Visualize it as a ball of crystalline light: crisp and clean, drawing closer to you. Visualize it filling the entire room, surrounding you, permeating you. Imagine it. Feel it. Visualize it. Remember that energy follows thought, so if you imagine it and focus upon it, it will manifest.

See within this ball of crystalline, colored light a doorway. Allow the form and shape of the door to come to mind. Let it take the shape of whatever is most suitable to you. It will differ from person to person. It is a door to your *own* subconscious.

The door opens inviting and welcoming you into the sphere of consciousness. The light and color within is even more brilliant and beautiful than what you first imagined. It is warm and comfortable and it permeates every aspect of your being. It takes you into it and you become a part of it.

Now repeat to yourself or out loud the God Name associated with that level. Think of the meaning of the God-Force that operates at this level of your being. Sound it slowly, emphasizing each syllable. Repeat it several times. Feel it echoing within your mind and carrying outside of you and surrounding you with its protective melody. Hear it sounding forth to the ends of the universe and then see the color become even more brilliant and crystalline, almost blinding in this state.

Now sound the name of the Archangel associated with the sphere. Feel the energy and color soften, becoming less intense and more bearable to your senses. Feel the protective span of the angelic wings surrounding you and protecting you. See it. Visualize it. Feel it. Make it manifest with the infinite power of your mind. Experience the infinite love and the infinite willingness to work with you to open yourself to the higher mysteries of your being.

As you vibrate the name of the Archangel of the sphere for the last time, something strange and wondrous begins to occur. The color shifts and waves like an early morning mist upon the river. As it clears, there forms before you an altar standing between two pillars. You are now within the temple of your consciousness.

These temples exist at every level. They are the same in many respects. They each have an altar. They each have two pillars, between which sits the altar. Upon the altar burns a lamp. It burns the color of the sphere. Other than this, each person's temple will differ. Whatever else may exist within the temple will vary with each person.

The temples are high and holy places. They are the places where you unite with all of mankind and life at that level—past, present and future. It is a place of tremendous energy and power. The pillars are a reminder for you to maintain balance as you touch the power and energy at that level. The lamp upon the altar is to remind you that the light of your potential and your own innate divinity burns perpetually within each person. And you are filled with awe and reverence for the love and magnificence of the Creator and at the love and magnificence within yourself that you have ignored and hidden.

It is then that you realize that you are not alone. At first it is more a feeling than anything else, but you remember that at this level all feelings have a basis in reality. As you gaze upon the altar, you see step from behind, as if out of a cloak of invisibility, a wondrous being.

There is associated with each level of consciousness, with each sephira, what has traditionally been called a "magical image." This magical image is the being that operates and works to transmit to you information and guidance from this level of your consciousness. Each level has its own "personage." This personage is more a thought-form than an actual being. The energy and work of all those seekers throughout the eons of time have allowed a build-up of energy that manifested these magnificent beings of energy. They share, often with the Archangels, the task of guide and mediator between us and this level of consciousness. And every level has its own being that operates in that function. Their image can reveal much about their level through meditation, and is well worth some individual attention along those lines. The table on page 95 lists the image and the sephira to which it is associated. It is this person of energy who steps from behind the altar.

A precautionary note needs to be inserted here. In the beginning you will be tapping these levels of consciousness on what is called an astral plane level. The astral plane of existence is occupied by beings other than just the higher forms. There are other lower life forms as well. Elementals and such operate upon this level. They of themselves are not evil, but they are quite capable of being mischievous and irresponsible. They are also capable of taking on the forms of that which we desire to see. They are master shapeshifters. It is also quite easy to be fooled in a territory whose laws and principles are new and unfamiliar to us. For this reason, after the magical image has appeared, you should again vibrate the God Name and the Archangelic Name. If there is deception going on, the image will break up and fade. If that does occur, simply continue vibrating the name until the correct image appears and remains.

Always test! One sitting does not make you an expert on that level, nor does it make you expert in recognizing deception at that level. It is very easy to be deceived and deluded. Remember that the virtue at the first level of consciousness, Malkuth, is the virtue of *discrimination*. That includes learning to discriminate between what is real and what is not, what is truth and what is deception and delusion. Flattery will be one of the most frequent types of delusion encountered. Test all things on these levels. There can appear symbols and elements within the temple experience that seem to make no sense. Test these as well by vibrating the God Name. If it doesn't dissolve afterwards, it is safe to assume that it is an aspect of that sphere, but an aspect that you have not yet encountered. That is *always* a good indication of your own growth and progress.

Treat every being encountered with courtesy. Deference and great respect should be given to superior orders of life such as the Archangels, Angels and rulers of the elements. To those who rank lower, including other humans who will from time to time be encountered, simply bear yourself as an equal. To the elementals and such, be polite, but firm and decisive. As said before, they can be mischievous and irresponsible, and they can "fairy charm" you if allowed. But there is no malice in them.

With common sense and some testing, there is no danger of encountering anything "evil." In fact, it will

Table of Magical Images within the Levels of Consciousness

Sephira	Magical Image
Kether	An ancient bearded king only seen in profile
Chokmah	A bearded male figure
Binah	A mature woman; matron
Chesed	A mighty crowned and throned king
Geburah	A mighty warrior in his chariot
Tiphareth	A majestic king; a child; a sacrificed god
Netzach	A beautiful naked woman
Hod	Hermaphrodite
Yesod	A beautiful naked man, very strong
Malkuth	a young woman, crowned and throned

make you stronger and more secure in seeking your higher natures. It is only when one is impatient and thinks he/she knows more than they do that trouble is encountered. Dabblers and curiosity seekers will be gravely disappointed, but those of an open mind, a willingness to put forth some effort toward their growth will find new worlds, higher truths and they will find themselves able to manifest greater joy, abundance, prosperity and light into their world.

As the image appears behind the altar, feel their love and willingness to work with you at this level and in whatever manner they can. Allow the person to speak to you. They know you. They will call you by name. They may even call you by names you have had before. Allow them to tell you how to work more easily and beneficially at that level. Listen to the advice. Ask questions when the opportunities to do so arrive. Allow it to unfold before you, and realize that it is more than just imagination.

Don't try and direct it too much, and don't try and make it follow some preconceived idea. Here you are only given an outline with which to work. The details of the outline will vary from individual to individual, and that is perfectly all right. There are books that give details on the beings at these levels, but do not limit yourself to those descriptions. Remember that we are trying to break down the old limitations. They may in fact have reason to appear to you in a manner quite different from the manner in which they are normally depicted. Do not be afraid to ask them why they appear in the manner they do. They will not be offended or insulted. They welcome the opportunity to teach and work with you more directly. After all, they have waited patiently for a long time just for such an occasion.

Allow them to end the session when they feel it is necessary. Thank the guide and ask if you may return. It is wrong to assume that one can visit with them any time. We don't like others making assumptions about us, and we certainly don't like visitors dropping in unannounced or uninvited. You will probably find that they extend an open invitation, but asking anyway is a simple courtesy and it helps to maintain a proper perspective and proper humility.

Step Five: Extracting the Energy

Having touched the level of consciousness and communicated with the higher beings at that level, now comes the task of bringing back that information and increased awareness to the normal state of consciousness. This is not difficult at all.

At the various levels of consciousness we must recognize that we are intimately connected to those beings who serve as mediators and teachers to us at those levels. We are, in fact, a part of them and they are, in fact, a part of us. And it is a level of our *own* consciousness. This means that what we learn at those various levels we can bring forth to our conscious levels and utilize to enhance our lives.

It is not just enough to touch the various levels within the Qabalistic Tree of Life. It is not just enough to touch the levels of our consciousness. That alone can be a wonderful experience, but it is incomplete by itself. Keep in mind that we are touching these levels to awaken within ourselves a greater awareness of our own innate divinity and power and to awaken a positive utilization of that power in our lives. We tap these levels to accelerate our growth and awareness. If we do not use what we learn from these levels, then it is wasted effort. We become mere dabblers in ancient wisdom.

There should be effort to utilize in some manner on a physical, normal, conscious state, the information tapped at the level *within one week*! The purpose for this is the completion of the circuit of the flow of energy. Only by reaching in, accessing the higher energies available and then utilizing them do we establish within our lives a balanced flow of that universal energy.

If we only tap the energy and awareness and do not utilize it, then we can create a build-up or damming of the energy. And because this is energy of a stronger, more vital power than we are used to tapping, this build-up can create extremely strong and negative imbalances within us and our lives. This can create emotional or mental imbalances of varying degrees, and can even manifest in situations in the physical environment that seem to be either chaotic or disturbing.

If we attempt to utilize the energy and awareness to some extent, then we open up a flow of energy that we can draw upon for greater and greater activities within our life. We open a wellspring of energy and power that is accessible to us at all times and can even work for us without our conscious awareness. The energy becomes "willing" to work for us at all times because it knows we wish and work to utilize it whenever we can. It is this kind of "underground" activity that makes for the wonderful surprises within our lives. It is the utilization that allows us to tap even greater and more powerful sources within us. It is what allows us to truly begin to take responsibility for our lives. It is what allows us to act in our lives rather than to be acted upon. It is what gives us control over the circumstances of our lives and thus leads us to the joy, fulfillment and abundance that we all desire and are capable of manifesting.

By inducing an altered state and following the steps outlined we not only open the various levels of our consciousness, but we do so through a manner that lays the foundation for even greater and more productive uses in the future. The guided imagery and the active imagination that we learn to employ through using the magical images help us to touch those levels of our being where lie certain archetypal symbols. Through the imagery, these archetypal energies can and will emerge. This is crucial to our overall growth and development. These symbols build a bridge between the subconscious and conscious mind. The symbols reflect what is the true reality within us and within the universe. By drawing it forth, by stimulating it to emerge, we have the opportunity to learn to utilize it and interpret it more consciously. We re-establish a "universal" bridge between our higher and lower selves. It is then that we open ourselves to the doorways of higher understanding and greater mysticism. When the conscious and subconscious minds work together, we then have access to *all* realms and *all* times.

We are then in essence using "fire to fight fire." We use the images that we call "magical" in conjunction with candles and essences to open the doors of the subconscious in order to retrieve even greater symbols. Symbology is the language of our unconscious self. It knows no other, and each of us at some time on our paths will have a need to learn to utilize it to a greater degree, to our fullest capability. If we intend to step out on the path of controlled and responsible higher evolution, we must become aware of the power and significance of symbols within our lives and within all aspects of our being.

Our lives are filled with symbols, but we do not want to confuse them with signs. Signs deal more with ordinary, mundane life. Symbols do as well, but they also contain inner, more archetypal meanings that have a capacity to lead us to greater awareness and higher realities. To understand symbols is to understand ourselves, including the deep-rooted and instinctive actions and capabilities. They help us to tap and understand the truths upon which our beliefs are based. They help us to open up to levels of our being that we have either ignored or have been unaware of their existence within us. *Symbols form the bridge that enables us to cross more dynamically from the rational to the progressive intuitive levels of our being. They assist the merging of the finite mind to the infinite.*

The symbols used in this method have universal meanings and derivations, but as individuals we will each place our own particular twist upon the symbols that we use and that we interpret. This is what makes the Tree of Life a *living tree*. In this manner, by not locking yourself rigidly into these guidelines, the symbols will touch both the objective and subjective realities of each individual.

Sometimes, what may emerge from this practice is information that we would rather not face. This is because as we go through life, we tend to form our own realities and we allow our energies to adjust to that reality and become complacent. This complacency which often manifests through our convictions and opinions keeps us from thinking and developing fully. Thus, the subconscious requires an even stronger symbol to shake the complacency and to break down the rigid, limiting patterns of thought and action within our lives. The procedure outlined is a safe and yet effective one for opening up the awareness of realities we ignore.

As we work with this technique, our awareness will grow and there will come a need for a change in the symbolism to a type that can even more effectively stimulate deeper responses. This is where the Qabalistic technique of "pathworking," accelerated learning, enters. It is a method of opening up and taking on karma and learning at an accelerated manner. More is discussed in Chapter Eight of this volume on the technique of pathworking in relation to the meditative procedure just outlined. As we begin with one and then expand to the other, we open to ourselves the option to proceed further into the sacred and transformative areas of the mind. This more than anything else will demonstrate how we each have the power of Alchemy over the conditions of our lives. *And that is when the magic emerges!*

Creating the Magical Body

A technique exists in ritual and ceremonial forms of invocation called the "Assumption of God Forms." Very simply, this is a method by which the participants within the ritual set up an energy within the temple that resonates with a particular god or goddess. Through the music, the prayers, the incense, the movements, through everything within the ceremony, the participants focus upon particular aspects of the god or goddess. The priest or priestess officiating within the ceremony builds an image of the God or Goddess, concentrates upon it to the exclusion of all else, so that he or she "becomes the God/Goddess," serving as a channel for those energies entering into the temple to be utilized by the participants.

This God Form is a representation of the force. It serves to set up resonance between the temple and that energy associated with the God/Goddess. This is, of course, a simplification, and there are many subtleties involved. If the proper God Form is chosen and developed, resonance will be established, and the force will pass through that form. The priest or priestess then is the mediator for that energy which is filtered into the consciousness and grounded within the temple for its particular purpose.

This is a process that occurs every Sunday within the Catholic church. During Communion in the service, the priest assumes a God Form. He becomes a representative of Jesus, a mediator for the Christ energy so that it can be distributed and shared in Communion with the congregation in the form of the wafer and the wine. In this is the significance of the words within the Mass: "Take this and eat of it for this is my body . . . Take thee and drink of this for this is my blood . . . " It is this assumption of the God Form that adds significance to the Master's admonition to his Apostles: "Do this in memory of me." By doing so, in memory, resonance with His energy is established and channeled to be utilized by them.

By learning to work with the energies of the Tree of Life through the method outlined earlier in this chapter you can begin to assume a new form. It may not be as powerful a method as can be utilized by one trained in the proper use of the assumption of God Forms, but it is a method that can develop into a realization that each and everyone is a son or daughter of God, and as such are heirs to *all* the energies within the universe.

By working with the positive images and energies associated with the different levels of consciousness, you stimulate a greater awakening of those energies within your life. Initially, they may not be as notice-able as you would like, but with persistence, they will demonstrate their availability and viability to all areas of your life. As you open yourself to these other levels of consciousness, you find that your old perceptions of yourself no longer fit. In the process of working with the Tree, you are creating a new image of your-self. This image begins to manifest and utilize the energies of greater strength, potential and benefit, derived from touching the various sephiroth. In es-sence, you are creating within your life your own *Magical Body*.

This Magical Body becomes a growing matrix of energy—new energy, released through touching those long-ignored levels of higher consciousness. This new energy becomes a blueprint for the manifestation and creation of new conditions within your life. As you touch each level of consciousness depicted within the Tree of Life, you add greater and newer energy to your Magical Body. As you continue to awaken and stimulate stronger energies, the time frame between the awakening upon the inner realms and the manifestation within your outer life of similar energies will diminish. With effort, this continues, until the Magical Body (and all of its inherent energies and powers) melds with your physical body (and all of its inherent powers and energies). The Magical Body augments your physical essence and experiences. You will not be able to do anything to one without it also affecting the other. If you speak ill, for example, of someone in the physical and you should not have, it will diminish the energy of your Magical Body. If you perform or speak or think positively in the physical, it will strengthen the Magical, and vice versa.

This process involves what is often termed the Principle of Correspondence: "As above, so below. As below, so above." Everything affects everything else. All levels and dimensions touch and are affected by all others.

One of the most beneficial activities an individual can participate in is the development of the Magical Body. In essence, it is utilizing spiritual alchemy to create a new you. When used in conjunction with the method described earlier in touching the powers of the sephiroth, it is a method that will place within your hands the opportunity and means of transmuting your energies, to strip away the dross of your life to reveal the gold that is the true *you*.

It begins by asking yourself questions and then visualize, imagine the answers. What is your highest self-image? What characteristics would it ideally have? Of what abilities and energies would you be the master? What would your appearance be? How would your appearance reflect the spiritual energies of which you are the master? How would being that way change how you act day-to-day at home? At work? Everywhere else in your life? If you could manifest those abilities now, how would you use them without allowing others to know? Imagine it. Contemplate upon it. Meditate upon it. Recognize that each time you touch one of those levels within the Tree of Life you add new power and new ability and new energy to your life. You are developing that Magical Body.

Spend time meditating upon what each of the sephira releases to you and how you will be able to use it the next day. Remember that the energy you touch at other levels of your consciousness has to be grounded, utilized within your physical life, or it is all for nothing. If you don't find a way to utilize it, you do not complete the process; you are only going halfway. That will create imbalance. If you are to complete the bridge between the conscious and the unconscious, you must utilize physical action. You must bring the inner images and energies to life within the physical.

You are a physical being. This means your primary focus should be within the physical. You can use other dimensions and levels of consciousness to augment the physical. If you don't utilize it within the physical, you create a build-up of intense energy that can create illness: physical, emotional, mental and/or spiritual. If you are to use other levels of consciousness for your betterment, then we need to learn to transform the energy of the inner to the outer world.

The Magical Body assists you in this process.

After touching the levels within the Tree, take some time over the next 24 hours to see how the Magical Body has grown. Visualize it as if it has achieved a new magical power or as if a Genie has released and granted a wish. See your image stronger and more vital, but also see how this new release will help you with something in your physical life. For example, imagine that you touched in with that level of the Qabala named Geburah. From Geburah, you can touch in with greater physical energy, strength, courage, etc. After touching in with that level of your consciousness, you would need to see yourself as stronger, more courageous. Form the image. Let it come to life. Imagine it! See it! Feel yourself stronger! Now visual ize yourself going through the day less tired, more vibrant, more vital. See others noticing how much more energetic you are.

Maybe you have been wanting to ask for a raise, but have been afraid. Visualize yourself doing so and receiving it. Then follow up on it the next day. Ask your employer for that raise. This will ground the energy you tapped in Geburah into the physical life. You may or may not get the raise initially, but you will have transferred the energy from the inner realm to the outer, building a bridge between them. Each time you do this thereafter, the bridge becomes stronger and the energy flows more fully, so that when you get ready to ask again, you will have more energy working for you to help manifest that raise.

One of the things that assists in this is to visualize yourself in the form that you have chosen for your Magical Body while you take the action to ground the energy into your physical life activities. As in the above example, seeing yourself strong with the energies of Geburah and full of magic and vitality before going in to ask for the raise triggers resonance with the energy you touched the night before in your meditation, stimulating it into action so you can use it in the physical.

You are creating a new you—*the ideal you*. Remember that you are not trying to change the old materialistic, physical you. You are awakening and creating, bringing to life, the *real you, the ideal you, the magical you*.

The more time and energy and effort you give to this process and to touching and awakening those energies, the quicker and stronger the response within your physical life. With each meditation and contemplation and imagination, be it on a particular level or ability within a level of your consciousness or be it upon your magical body, you are planting a *seed thought*. A seed thought means that if you put a magical or mystical idea into your visualization and creative imagination and build it clearly and with strong intention, it will grow in energy and strength. You must recognize that this process is a reflection of the Divine operating within you. If you repeat this process with strong intention every day, for even just a few moments, these seeds will form a bridge to the Divine that will enhance and energize every aspect of your life. It will increase your creativity and your expression of it while in the physical.

These seed thoughts grow into living thought-forms of energy. A thought-form is a thought or idea that takes on a particular shape or form when given energy by your thinking and your feeling. This thought-form can work for good or for ill. Negative thoughts and feelings will create negative thought-forms working for you; positive thoughts and feelings will create positive thought-forms working for you. You are trying to discipline your energies, bring them under control. Creating the thought-form for the Magical Body assists in this. Its strength will be determined by the intensity of your thoughts and feelings and the length of time the thoughts are perpetuated. They can exist within your aura to supplement your energies throughout the day and they can even be developed to the point where they can become more independent, able to travel through the ethers to help set things and energy into motion for you while you are otherwise occupied.

The power that you *imagine* on the inner planes transfers to the outer. You become active in the creation of your life circumstances. You become a creative power. If you can imagine it, then it *does* exist at some level of your being. And if it already exists, then it simply needs to be channeled and directed into those areas of your life in which you want it.

You need to keep in mind only one thing. In a universe of infinite energies and life forms, anything that can expand your consciousness can only benefit you. By opening yourself to the possibility first, and then the actuality, you open yourself to wonders and worlds waiting to be explored. You open yourself to the mysteries of life, and you create greater opportunity for fulfillment, prosperity and joy within your individual life expressions.

By touching the powers of the sephiroth, you assist in the formulation of your Magical Body. The Magical Body is a reflection, a growing, changing, expanding reflection of the God/Goddess within you. It will take the form and energy that you wish and develop. It will manifest as the divine you, inherent with all the powers and abilities of Divinity. And at the same time, it will become uniquely *you*. There will be similarities with others, but your expression and manifestation of those energies will be unique. That is what makes magic so wondrous. It is why the Tree is such a dynamic symbol for the Qabala. Every tree has similarities. They have bark, leaves, roots, limbs, and yet each one is unique. Each grows in its own creative and individual manner.

The tree is a very ancient symbol. Primitive peoples saw the tree as that which separated the heavens from the earth, and at the same time it served as a bridge between the two. By touching the powers and forming the Magical Body you are becoming a living tree. Your roots are within the Earth, but your branches touch the heavens. You are comprised of energies of both, with room in between to grow to heights not even imagined.

Other Methods

As you begin to work with the various levels within your consciousness as depicted within the Qabala, you will find that you will adapt the methods described in here to suit you. This is how it should be. Part of your responsibility in accelerating your evolvement is learning to utilize and express energies in the way that is uniquely individual. You are being presented with guidelines to assist in the opening up to higher potential. They are not strict, nor will they be suitable for everyone, but there are benefits to be derived from them.

Utilizing the techniques can assist your development in a variety of ways. The Qabala can be used to:

1. Point out personality issues and fears.
2. Lead to sources of anxiety and ways of dealing with stress.
3. Fill you with creative ideas and energy potential.
4. Offer alternative ways of perceiving situations and of acting in the world.
5. Explore past life experiences in relation to current life experiences.
6. Inspire and entertain.
7. Open you to the magnificence of the inner world.
8. Offer the opportunity to participate in the arena of the unconscious.
9. Prevent you from becoming too caught up in your outer life.
10. Help articulate life's journey.
11. Mirror the soul and its growth.
12. Offer ways of harmonizing the outer and the inner worlds.
13. Heal yourself and others on all levels.
14. Connect with spiritual teachers and guides.
15. And yet other ways.

Several of these will be explored in greater detail in Volume Two. It is not always good to provide too many different techniques in the beginning because they only serve to confuse the beginner. One technique that does deserve further exploration is utilizing the Qabala to heal.

As you begin to work and touch the different levels of your consciousness, you will realize that each level dominates a particular part of your physical or emotional being. Earlier in this work, the mundane associations of the various sephiroth were discussed. Planetary associations were given. In astrology, certain parts of the physical body are associated with the different planets. Thus, if you know what level of your consciousness connects into the energy linked with the planet and its corresponding energy in the physical body, you can tap that level to assist and accelerate the healing. If a particular area of the body is out of balance, you can bring it into balance by touching in with that level of your consciousness. For example, if there is a problem within the heart and lung area of the body, this could indicate a Sun or Moon influence or imbalance. The Sun rules the heart and lungs, and the Moon rules the lungs and stomach.

You could then connect with those energies in the Tree of Life that are reflected in the Sun or the Moon. For the Sun, connect with that level called Tiphareth; for the moon, connect with the level of Yesod.

The process for releasing the healing energies at those levels of consciousness is simple. Follow the procedure outlined earlier in this chapter for opening that level of your consciousness to you. As the magical image appeared, you would discuss what the cause of the problem is and how to correct it in the physical.

Two methods that I have found effective for releasing healing energies are as follows: I have had asthma since I was a child. As I grew older, I found that emotional situations served to trigger "attacks." For this reason, when I work to alleviate the condition through the energies of the Tree of Life, I usually choose to touch in with Yesod. The Moon rules emotions, and the moon's energies are reflected through the sephira of Yesod.

As I speak with either the Archangel or the magical image, I allow them to assist me in discovering what emotions I have allowed to affect me and thus manifest the condition of asthma. Many times I do not want to accept what I hear, but through further contemplation and analysis, I usually realize that what I was told was correct, and in all cases, I allowed it to manifest. By touching in with this level, concerning this problem, I was placed in a position of having to take greater responsibility.

I then allow the energy at that level to restore balance to my lungs. This usually takes the form of one of two ways. I follow my own intuition as to which way feels right at the time. In the first, I visualize the light upon the altar growing in intensity—almost blinding in its brilliance. I see it. I feel it. I imagine it burning away the feelings that have congested the lungs. I feel the energy of the light permeate me, filling me with healing energy, restoring balance to my body. I "release" the energy that burns within my own consciousness at that level to work for me. This provides relief until I can take whatever steps are necessary in the physical to deal with and cleanse myself of the cause.

The second way is to allow the Archangel to provide the healing energy. I have found this to be more effective and a uniquely different experience in the healing process. I visualize this great being of Light stepping up to me and touching me, blessing me. I feel myself enveloped in the love and strength that flows unconditionally and freely to me and through me, restoring balance and health. I am usually speechless at this point, but I always mentally thank this wondrous being.

This, of course, does not take the place of doctors or the need for them within your life, but it does give you a way of beginning to take greater responsibility for your health and well-being, and that means you must realize that if you have an illness, you created and focused the energy that allowed it to manifest. And if you created it, then you can change it! The following chart shows some of the correspondences between various illnesses and aches and pains and the levels of your subconscious in which you can begin to correct the conditions. Remember, you are starting to learn how to touch other dimensions and levels of yourself. As you work at it, greater will be the rewards. In Volume Two, even stronger methods of tapping healing energy will be explored.

Healing Energies Within the Tree

Sephira	Correspondence to the Physical Body
Malkuth (Earth)	Where all illness manifests
Yesod (Moon)	Breasts, lungs, ovaries, stomach, menstruation, all emotional-based illnesses
Hod (Mercury)	Nervous system, hands, vocal cords, thyroid, respiration, solar plexus, mental problems
Netzach (Venus)	Physical attractiveness, hair, skin, kidneys, reproductive system, thymus, complexion
Tiphareth (Sun)	All general health problems, heart, back, blood pressure, circulation, stamina, spine
Geburah (Mars)	Energy, anemia, colds, red corpuscles, muscular system, sinuses, adrenals, temperature
Chesed (Jupiter)	Liver, hips, thighs, intestines, cell nutrition, formation of hemoglobin
Binah (Saturn)	Skin, bones, joints, teeth, spleen, hearing, tendons, colds, congestion
Chokmah (Solar System)	Left side of face, balancing hemispheres, sinuses, pituitary gland
Kether (Universe)	Cranium, crown chakra

Use of Imagination

Many may believe that these methods are all in one's "imagination" and have no basis in reality. It is wrong to assume that the imagination is illusion, or worse, delusion. Those who would find fault are simply revealing their own fears, and for them, this technique is not recommended. As mentioned earlier, the Qabala has the tremendous capacity for revealing our greatest potentials and our greatest *fears*, and if an individual is not willing to confront both aspects, avoidance of the "magical" path of evolvement is to be recommended.

There are many who fear contact with any energy, life or power outside of the physical. Usually, the ones who are so vehement concerning this are the ones who also fear contact with other humans outside of their own race, religion, sex, etc. We each have the capacity to set limits upon the relationships we form with energies and life-forms operating in the inner dimensions, just as we have the capacity to set limits upon the relationships with those in our physical lives.

Yes, there are negative and ignorant energies in the so-called spiritual realms, the inner planes of life, just as there are in the physical. This does not preclude trying to develop relationships with those who can benefit us and help us to awaken to our highest and greatest expression of life. We would not hide in our homes, afraid to make any contact with other humans simply because we have heard there were bad people walking around. We alone decide who we allow into our lives—in the physical and in the spiritual.

We have the control. Working with the Qabala not only demonstrates how much control, but shows us how to increase it within our physical lives.

It begins by learning to work with the energies of the subconscious. It is not only the storehouse for all of our most powerful expressions of energy, but it also serves as a bridge to all other forces, energies *and life forms within the universe.* The keys to tapping and releasing these perceptions and energies is through that which is called the *imagination.* It is the process of creating images within the mind. It is the faculty of producing ideal creations consistent with reality. We could not create the images unless there was a connection to something in reality, be it a physical reality or a spiritual one. If it did not exist in some form on some level, we would not be able to imagine it.

Science knows that our subconscious controls around 90 per cent of our body's functions. It carries on its work without any conscious direction by us. Science also knows that we each only utilize a fractional part of our brain power. If we can learn to direct the subconscious energies to a greater degree with our conscious mind/brain, we could open up potentials and abilities that would enable us to impact our physical environments to a much greater degree, shaping them more consciously in the manner that would be more beneficial to us. We could create greater prosperity, fulfillment, abundance and love within them. We would do the acting, rather than being acted upon. We would find that we are not at the mercy of our circumstances.

This creative process involves disciplined use of the imagination. It requires learning to focus and concentrate upon images that open up our subconscious energies to conscious control. The conditons of our lives are of our own creation. We wrote the scripts. We formed the images that became the matrix, the blueprint of energy, for the formulation and manifestation of all we experience within our lives. Our doubts, our worries and our fears are all negative, limiting uses of the imagination. It actually serves to manifest and augment the negative experiences of our lives. It is often said that "Faith will move mountains." Faith, the process of seeing something (imaging it) as a reality within your life, can work for us or against us. Doubts and fears and the images they create are forms of negative faith.

We are better off with no imagination than one that works against us. If our dreams and doubts and fears rise over and over again to defeat us, we need to bring it under disciplined use. The imagination is a *tool*. By learning to direct the imagination to things that are expansive and fulfilling, rather than depriving, we become the masters of our existence.

It is the destiny of man to conquer matter, to master the physical. This does not mean that we use methods to escape or seek out a blinding, heavenly light in the spiritual from which there is no return. Our task is to bring the spiritual into the physical—the spiritualization of matter.

A creative person is one who can process information in new ways; take whatever they can find from whatever source they can find and reshape it and resynthesize it into what works for them as an individual. A creative person *imaginatively* sees ways of transforming ordinary experiences into unique and new expression.

New discoveries concerning the operation of the mind and brain are providing new insights into the ancient "magical" methods of releasing creative potential. Inside our skulls we have a double brain, each with its own way of knowing. Their distinct characteristics demonstrate with increasing clarity the use and development of altered states of consciousness in that process of releasing higher potentials. The left hemisphere is more logical, more rational in its approach to assimilating and utilizing information. It analyzes, counts, follows step-by-step procedures. It is sequential in its approach to learning.

The right hemisphere differs in its processing. We "see" things that may be imaginary (existing in the mind's eye) or recall things that may or may not be real. Through the efforts of the right hemisphere, we see how things exist in space, how parts go together. Through it we dream, understand metaphors and symbols and create new combinations of ideas. Through the right hemisphere, we use and tap intuition and experience leaps of insight.

One of the marvelous capabilities of the right hemisphere is imaging: seeing a picture, symbol or image with the mind's eye. The mind is able to conjure up an image and examine it. These images reflect sensory information and data: past (including past lives), present and future. Through the right hemisphere, we can take various sensory data and see it in relation to anything we desire. It is for this reason that symbols, visualization and creative imagination are a part of developing higher potential. They assist us in accessing those levels of consciousness that are most easily accessible to us through the right hemisphere of the brain. Learning to utilize it in a controlled and directed manner, to access deeper insights and energies and then to bring it out and put it to use in some aspect of our life (a process that is often left brain), is all part of that process of using creative imagination. It assists us in using both sides of the brain to access and implement greater levels of energy and consciousness within our lives.

Working with the symbology and imagery within the Tree of Life assists us in this. It gives us a method of opening deeper levels of consciousness through the right hemisphere of the brain and then bring the energies out to play within our day-to-day life through the left hemisphere. This enables us to utilize our imagination and focus its strength on creating the positive within our life rather than that which limits and repeats itself. It helps draw us into positive aspects and energies.

To achieve results and tap deeper levels of our consciousness and greater potentialities, we need to be able to shift our awareness and then control and maintain it for the time and purpose necessary. Controlled and active visualization, imagination and meditation is a learned and creative skill. It can be learned and utilized by all. Just as some individuals learn to read much more easily and quickly than others, the same holds true for utilizing creative imagination. *But all can learn it!*

As with all learned skills, it does require practice and persistence. The more we practice, *the more energy, power and magic will manifest into our lives.*

Chapter 7

Strengthening and Protecting Techniques

Invoke often; Enflame thyself with prayer!
The Sacred Magic of Abramelin
the Mage

The human being is basically an energy system. He or she takes in energy and then transmutes it to be used for varying purposes. As energy is taken in and awakened within us, it emanates from the physical body. This energy emanation from the body is called the *aura*. The aura shows what we are experiencing on all levels as well as what we have already experienced.

The aura surrounds us in every direction. It is three dimensional. It is comprised of varying levels of density and intensity. The further one moves away from the physical body, the more subtle and the more difficult it is to see the aura.

Everyone needs to learn to recognize the limits and strengths of their own energy fields, their auric fields. We each need to be aware of when there may be a need to intensify our energy fields, strengthen them, purify and cleanse them of negativity. Every time our aura contacts the aura of someone else, there is an exchange of energy. Every time when things get hectic, emotional or extra "mental," when situations and people around us aggravate, irritate or bother us, we give off and use more energy from our own field.

We need to recognize when we are losing and using excessive amounts of energy. We need to recognize and learn how to recharge that energy before we deplete it to the stage where an illness may manifest. We need to become as familiar with our energy field as we are with the actions of our bodies. By doing so, we can stop our energies from leaking out needlessly, and prevent others from taking our energy. We can then cleanse our fields of the extraneous and often negative energies that our aura accumulates throughout the day simply through contact with other people.

By awakening and utilizing all the energies at all levels of our beings in a balanced manner, our energy field remains vibrant and strong. We then have greater reservoirs to tap and we improve our health: physical, emotional, mental and spiritual.

We have the essence of all energies in unlimited amounts within our being. We are, in fact, a reflection in miniature of all the universal energies. We are the microcosm of the universe. We are, in fact, the Tree of Life! As we awaken and utilize all aspects of our being, all energies within the Tree, we create an energy field around us that is vibrant, strong and protective. It shields us from negativity and increases our own energy levels to the point where we can tap and utilize even greater amounts.

When we don't use our energies to their fullest capabilities, misuse them and abuse them, or awaken them in unbalanced manners, our Tree does not grow. It begins to wither and weaken. Our energy is depleted and we have less resistance to those things which can create harm to us, and we also have less energy to manifest what we need and desire in our lives. It is at those times that we are at the mercy of our life circumstances. It is then that we find ourselves in situations that are less than ideal. We have, in essence, allowed our energies to leak through or energy field. We have created "auric wounds," punctures and holes within our energy field that permits our energy to leak out or not accumulate quickly nor strongly enough to reinstate balance and well-being *on all levels of our lives!*

There are various things and activities that assist in the creation of auric wounds: wounds that allow our energies to seep out and not to be used to optimum. Drugs, alcohol, mental and emotional trauma all are capable of creating wounds and sapping our energies. Unwise meditations—the kind in which manipulation of people and events occur—also can create wounds. Stress and tobacco also assist in depleting our energies.

We must remember that if we are to tap our highest inner resources we must be in a state of emotional, mental and physical health that permits the most balanced use of them. We tap the other levels to help us fulfill and accelerate our growth in the physical, but we are in the *physical*. For that reason, we must take care to keep our physical vehicle in as good con-

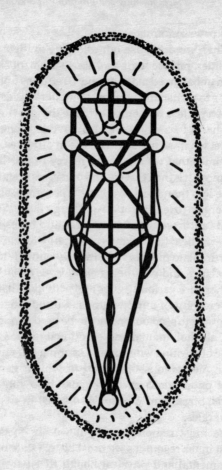

The Tree of Life Within the Aura

dition as possible. We use the Qabala as a system for growth and increased awareness. We use it to take back upon ourselves the responsibility for our lives. Part of the responsibility is the proper care of our physical being. We must always balance the physical, emotional, mental and spiritual states. They *all* must work together. To ignore one for the others creates imbalance. If we are doing so, work with the Qabala will make that quite evident. It is then that we must take responsibility and the steps necessary to reinstill the balance. It is then that we are truly awakening the Tree of Life within us.

Traditionally there are two techniques for working with the energies in the Qabala that assist in the process of not only awakening the energies, but strengthening them and protecting them as well. They are two techniques or exercises that the beginner should learn and utilize as often as possible. The first is the use of the *Qabalistic Cross* and the second is the *Middle Pillar Exercise*. Both strengthen, balance and protect one's energies.

The Qabalistic Cross

The Qabalistic cross is a form of the sign of the cross with which most Christians are familiar. It must be noted that the Qabalistic cross predates the Christian cross. The cross is a universal and archetypal symbol. It touches the subconscious of every being at some point within their development. It can be found in almost all religions, and was taught in all the ancient Mystery Schools. There are many associations to it: the four cardinal points of the universe, the four elements, the four Archangels, etc. It is used by the

Qabalist to awaken the higher life flow of energies within his being. Learning to utilize it and "build" it into the aura is one of the primary steps of the seeker to higher knowledge.

The Qabalistic cross is a means of awakening your inner spiritual light and calling it forth into action. It is a means of alerting all of your spiritual centers in the Tree of Life that you are going to begin to activate them. It stabilizes the entire aura and protects you, so that you can more fruitfully access those spiritual centers.

As with all the exercises in this book, you will util ize visualization and sound to manifest the power within the exercise—the power within you. Stand facing East, if possible, with your feet together, shoulders back and your arms at your side. Then take several deep breaths from the diaphragm. As you inhale and exhale slowly, visualize yourself growing and expanding up through the top of your house, into the clouds, until you are standing upon the Earth itself with the entire universe before you and around you. Feel it, imagine it, visualize it and it will be!

With your thumb to represent your inner Divine Spirit, your first finger to represent the creative fire within you and the universe, and your middle finger to represent the calling forth of the other two to the earth plane, touch your forehead between the eyes and vibrate slowly the Hebrew word ATEH (Ah-Toh). Give equal emphasis to each syllable and visualize the sounds carrying forth to the ends of the universe. As you touch your forehead, visualize a brilliant explosion of light manifesting around your head and extending upward into infinity.

Bring the thumb and fingers slowly down, drawing the light down into you and touch the center of your chest. Vibrate the word MALKUTH (Mahl-Kuth). Malkuth is at the bottom of the Tree of Life and thus within the body. It is associated with the area around the feet. It is awkward to bend down and touch the feet. Because of this, touch the heart area. The heart is the center of your being and from it you can reach any other area. Visualize the light extending down to the feet, exploding in brilliant, crystalline light and then extending downward to infinity. You now have created a beam of universal energy extending through you to infinity in two directions.

Now bring the thumb and fingers to the right shoulder. Visualize again the explosion of crystalline light and see the light extending out from the right shoulder into infinity. Vibrate the words VE-GEBURAH (Veh-Geh-Bur-Ah). Then draw the line of light across the chest to touch the opposite shoulder.

As you touch the left shoulder, visualize and feel that brilliant explosion of light. Vibrate the words VE-GEDULAH (Veh-Geh-Du-Lah) and visualize the light extending from the shoulder out into infinity also.

At this point raise both arms to the side, palms upward. Bow the head and bring the hands to a folded position at the chest, fingers pointing upward and vibrate the words LE-OLAM AMEN (Leh-Oh-Lahm Ah-men). At this point you should visualize yourself as a being of tremendous light and energy, balanced and brilliant, shining in all directions.

Through the visualization and the vibrating of the words, you have called upon the energies within you and the Divine without to transmute yourself into a cross of brilliant light.

The words are very significant as they are both Qabalistic and Christian. They are part of the Lord's Prayer. They are the words that the Master Jesus passed on to his followers. They are words that demonstrate His knowledge of this Ancient and Holy system of development:

ATEH	= THINE IS
MALKUTH	= THE KINGDOM
VE-GEBURAH	= AND THE POWER
VE-GEDULAH	= AND THE GLORY
LE-OLAM	= FOREVER
AMEN	= AMEN.

Vibrate the names and words strongly—if need be, several times. This not only improves concentration, but it can help you to formulate the cross more clearly and vividly. You want the cross (and thus yourself) to be so brilliant that it is blinding in its intensity and so that it actually lights up the universe. The sounds and the visualizations evoke tremendous power and energy within you. Remember that this is a holy process and deserves attention and reverence.

The Qabalistic Cross should be used before any meditation or ritual work. It stabilizes the aura and protects. It should also be used after meditations and touchings within other levels of consciousness, so that the other areas are closed and sealed and we are fully grounded back on the earth plane. It can be used during the day when things get hectic, people pres-

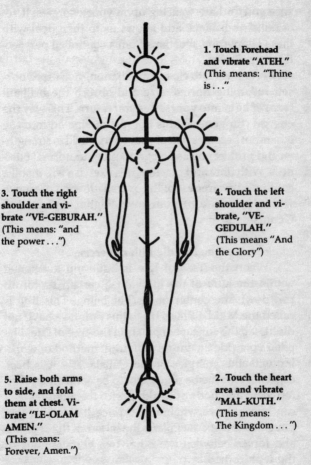

1. Touch Forehead and vibrate "ATEH." (This means: "Thine is . . .")

3. Touch the right shoulder and vibrate "VE-GEBURAH." (This means: "and the power . . .")

4. Touch the left shoulder and vibrate, "VE-GEDULAH." (This means "And the Glory")

5. Raise both arms to side, and fold them at chest. Vibrate "LE-OLAM AMEN." (This means: Forever, Amen.")

2. Touch the heart area and vibrate "MAL-KUTH." (This means: The Kingdom . . .")

Qabalistic Cross

sure you and are wearing upon your energies. It re-establishes balance and allows us to then deal with these people and situations from a controlled perspective as possible.

When used to close a meditation, visualize yourself resuming normal size and absorb the brilliant cross of light into yourself as you return. This way the energy you generated is not just dissipated into the ethers but becomes part of your energy field to strengthen and protect you as you go about your normal business. With time and practice, this exercise will instill a continued awareness of the overshadowing presence within your life of your own Higher and Divine Genius.

The Middle Pillar Exercise

When the Tree of Life is built and awakened within the aura of the individual, certain sephiroth run down the center of his/her being. This line is called the Middle Pillar. Up to this point we have not discussed the concept of pillars in the Tree of Life. The pillars provide an entirely different method of working with the energies of the Qabala, and it is best, especially for the beginner, not to be confronted with too many methods of working with the energies as it can become overwhelming. Suffice it to say at this point that the Middle Pillar is the *balance* of the energies and forces between the other two vertical lines of the sephiroth.

The Middle Pillar exercise is one which taps these balancing energies and builds them into the aura. This exercise pumps such tremendous amounts of energies into the aura that it seals leaks, holes and such that may exist within it. It stabilizes the entire energy field of the individual and increases the energy within it to the extent that we have greater amounts with which to work during our normal course of events in the day. It prevents an overtapping of our psychic, physical, emotional, mental and spiritual energies. This exercise also heightens the awareness of our own Higher Self overshadowing us. It is an exercise that beginners and high initiates can draw benefit from, for it has possibilities that only practice will reveal.

The Middle Pillar in the Tree of Life consists of four spheres or four levels of consciousness: Kether, Tiphareth, Yesod and Malkuth. As we open ourselves to the energies within and continue our growth and study, we will become aware of the fact that there is actually a fifth sephira within the Middle Pillar. It is called Daath, the invisible sephira. This is actually an eleventh level of consciousness existing within us. It is the level of hidden knowledge which helps us bridge the gaps in our growth and our consciousness. For the beginner, it is enough to know that it exists and that it can also be utilized just as the others can. It forms a part of the Middle Pillar exercise and is thus located between Kether and Tiphareth.

By including the hidden level of consciousness within the Middle Pillar exercise, we are able to tap some very ancient symbolism. Five is the number for the senses, what we use in our normal level of consciousness, but five is also symbolic of the one sense hidden (Daath) behind the five senses, that sixth sense which will enable us to touch our Higher Selves. The five spheres can also represent the five elements: the FIRE of creativity, the WATER of perpetual life, the EARTH of our foundation, the AIR of our higher knowledge, and the Divine SPIRIT operating behind them all. Through the Middle Pillar exercise, we tap all of the elements and awaken their energies within us in a balanced manner—enabling the optimum use of them.

You can begin the exercise in either a standing or seated position. As in the previous exercises, you will utilize visualization and sound. As in all the others as well, begin with the Qabalistic cross to stabilize the energy field. It is beneficial at this point to utter some prayer of devotion to the higher divine energies that you will be tapping. The prayer can be of your own choosing, but it should not be something which is spoken in a deadpan and rote manner. You should be able to feel the words as you speak them and visualize them echoing forth into the universe to your Divine Source.

Next, visualize a brilliant crystalline white sphere forming just atop of your head. It is vibrant and alive with energy. Imagine it vibrating and shimmering with brilliance. This is the energy from the level of Kether that you are drawing upon and bringing into manifestation within your being. At this point you vibrate the name of the God Force that is linked to this level of consciousness and being: EHEIEH (Eh-Huh-Yeh). As you repeat the name, emphasize each syllable and visualize the sphere of light becoming even more brilliant and powerful, filling the crown of your head with energy. There is no set number of times to repeat the name. Use it as a mantram, repeating it until your own *intuition* tells you to go on. The sounding of the names does not have to be loud, and can even be accomplished silently with practice.

When this sphere of light feels sufficiently activated (it is important to learn to trust your feelings in this matter), visualize a shaft of light just as brilliant and blinding descend down through the head to the neck and throat area. This is the level of Daath. At this level visualize a second sphere of light, bringing it into manifestation through your thoughts.

We have not discussed the various associations and energies found in the level of consciousness that we refer to as Daath. The God-Force that is active within its level is a balance between the God-Force of Chokmah and the God-Force of Binah. For this reason, we use a name that encompasses both aspects: YHVH ELOHIM (Yah-Hoh-Voh Eh-Loh-Heem). As you vibrate this name, the sphere of light also vibrates, growing in intensity and brilliance until you feel it unmistakenly active in your neck area.

Then visualize the shaft of light descending from the bottom of the second sphere to form into a third sphere in the heart area of your being. This is the sphere of Tiphareth. Remember that with all the spheres they are multi-dimensional and they extend outward to the front and to the back of you as well. Imagine this sphere of Light. Feel it. Know that it is being brought into manifestation through the concentration of your thoughts and the sound of the Divine Name of Power.

Vibrate the name YHVH ELOAH VaDAATH (YAH-Hoh-Voh Eh-Loh-Ah Va-Dah-Ahth). Feel it echo

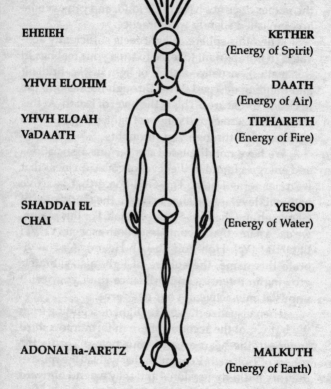

EHEIEH — **KETHER** (Energy of Spirit)

YHVH ELOHIM — **DAATH** (Energy of Air)

YHVH ELOAH VaDAATH — **TIPHARETH** (Energy of Fire)

SHADDAI EL CHAI — **YESOD** (Energy of Water)

ADONAI ha-ARETZ — **MALKUTH** (Energy of Earth)

The Middle Pillar Exercise

within you and to the ends of the universe. See the sphere vibrate and grow in intensity with each repetition of the Divine Name. Feel the energy pouring down from the crown of the head into the heart area, filling you with light and energy.

Visualize the shaft of light descending from the bottom of this sphere to form the fourth in the area of the groin. Feel the sphere come alive with energy and brilliance as you vibrate the name of the God-Force that rules that level—SHADDAI EL CHAI (Shah-Dye-El-Cheye). Imagine, feel and recognize the activity of the energy—alive and vibrant within this area of your being.

Finally, visualize the shaft of light descending from the bottom of the fourth sphere down to the feet. Here it forms the fifth of the spheres of energy that constitute the Middle Pillar. Vibrate the name ADONAI ha-ARETZ (Ah-Doh-Nye hah-Ah-Retz). This awakens the highest and most spiritual energy at that level of consciousness and draws it into activity in the area of your feet. Feel it whirling and vibrating with greater and greater intensity and brilliance as you repeat the name.

It is at this point that you have not only awakened a tremendous amount of spiritual energy, but you have also manifested it within your organism. Pause for a moment as you feel the five spheres of spiritual energy shining along the shaft of light that permeates your body. At this point there is only one step left, and that is the circulation of this energy to encompass your entire being and its energy field.

With the spheres and the shaft shining brilliantly,

draw your attention back to the sphere at the crown of the head. It is at this point that you utilize rhythmic breathing to circulate energy. As you exhale slowly, see and feel the energy pour into the top sphere and then stream down the left side of the body. Feel the left side fill with this light energy and radiate outward, strengthening your aura on that side. As you inhale slowly, draw the energy up the right side of the body, filling it and radiating outward into your aura on that side. Feel your aura expand and strengthen with each breath. Continue this until you can feel the circulation of this energy around your body and your aura. See it. Feel it. Know that you bring it into being with the infinite power of your mind. This forms a broad electromagnetic field of energy around you giving you an aura of strength and light. Repeat several times.

Next, as you exhale, allow the energy to pour down the front of you. It is strong and brilliant and fills your aura to overflowing. As you inhale, draw the energy up the back of you. Continue with this until you feel it circulating and expanding with increased strength and brilliance. You now have strong circulating energy around your entire being. Pause, simply visualize and feel the energy around you. Know that it has sealed any leaks. Know that it has replaced any lost energy. Know that it has filled your aura and your entire being with a light-energy that is intense, brilliant and healthful.

Allow the energy to gather at the foot center. Visualize the shaft of light that radiates through all the spheres as a hollow tube of light. As you inhale, feel the energy being drawn up the tube to the head center, and as you exhale, feel the infinite energy shower forth throughout your entire being to be drawn back up through the bottom again and out the top. Visualize it as a rainbow of intense energy droplets streaming forth from your head, showering your entire essence in brilliant and blinding colors of energy. Continue at least five times and allow your being to bask and shimmer in its new found energy and light.

End the exercise with a brief prayer or even a brief meditation or contemplation upon the brilliance of your being. Ground your energies, drawing them into your being with the Qabalistic cross, confident in the strength and protection from such powerful spiritual energy. You have become a being of Light!

Variations

There are many variations and adaptations to the Middle Pillar exercise. Some sources and books will list an entirely different cosmology to the various sephiroth. Some may list Greek and Roman gods and goddesses in connection with the sephiroth, while others may assign Egyptian deities to them. One is not better than another. They all serve their purposes. It must be remembered that the energies evoked with different names will resonate within us differently.

One of the more common variations of the Middle Pillar exercise is to activate six centers rather than the five. The sixth is a combined intoning of the names for Binah and Chokmah forming a brilliant, crystalline light in the area of the brow or "third eye." This further stimulates greater clairvoyance. There is often discussion and mild disagreement as to which God Name will activate this particular center. The key, of course, is not to lock yourself into what other sources decree. Experiment. Remember the Qabala teaches us greater responsibility in our lives. Intoning the God Name JEHOVAH does stimulate this center. Since the God Name for Binah is Jehovah Elohim and the God Name for Chokmah is JAH or JEHOVAH, JEHOVAH has always seem suitable for this particular variation.

This variation also serves to trigger a chakra balance and activation. It does so for our major energy distribution centers:

> **EHEIEH—Crown Chakra,** Soul purpose,
>   link with God
> **JEHOVAH—Brow Chakra,** Imagination,
>   clairvoyance energies
> **JEHOVAH ELOHIM—Throat Chakra,**
>   Creative expression, clairaudience
> **JEHOVAH ALOAH VA DAATH—Heart**
>   **Chakra,** Healing ability, love,
>   immune energies
> **SHADDAI EL CHAI—Base Chakra,**
>   Health, intuition, kundalini energy
> **ADONAI HA ARETZ—Feet Chakra,**
>   Grounding of spiritual energies

It does not matter which variation we utilize, as long as we recognize the significance of the energies which we are awakening. Regardless of whether we attach a Roman or Hebrew cosmology to the Tree of Life, we need to be aware of the intricacies of the energies we awaken. Those in the Western world will have a stronger resonation within themselves to the Hebraic system, although we are by no means limited to it.

To more fully understand this, we need to recognize the Qabala in its Hebraic form as being what is termed the *Western Occult Tradition*. This implies that for those in the West, the assignation of Hebraic names and references will resonate most strongly with the levels of consciousness we are attempting to touch. It is necessary to recognize the power that has been added to the Qabala (including the thought-forms associated with it) has come about most strongly through the Christ. Since that time, the energies that resonate within all of us have altered tremendously, and it is necessary to be aware of it in order to open and develop ourselves to the fullest.

Remember that the educator for all of the souls within this solar system is the one who is referred to as the Cosmic Christ. Because of the scope of New Age energies that would be unfolded, it was necessary to do everything possible to unfold from humanity and nourish the strong seeds of a consciousness of truth and love, prior to the onset of the Seventh Ray and Aquarian Age energies of which Qabalistic ritual would become a part. Much of the special evolution which the Earth stimulates in man is in learning to deal with the dense conditions of energy—in learning the creative possibilities of limitation while at the same time learning how to transcend limitations (which can also be reflected through study of the Qabala). This required the spiritual being (such as man) who sought such evolution to express through a physical body.

The "Fall of Man" was the original alignment of

his spiritual energies with the forces of materialization so that he could enter into physical existence. Although a sacrifice, it provided and prepared the way for an expanded expression of the spirit and consciousness once he graduated from this creative density. This process was possible because of the action of certain "materialization" forces which weigh the being down. It added the element of gravity to the energy expression of us.

There was risk though. If the consciousness became too involved with the energies of gravity and materialization—the forces that pull downward into density— then the soul runs the risk of not being able to rise properly. Mankind became too involved with the energies and beings of materialization and ran the risk of becoming entrapped in the realms of matter and form. When the time came for the consciousness to grasp and receive the higher energies, man/woman was unable to do so. The stimulation of the higher faculties could not occur as fully and thus lift each soul back into the realm of spirit as *Masters of Evolution*, a time represented by the New Age.

Man became too focused on gathering experiences and forgot his/her true home on higher levels. His/her character reflected the characteristics of matter (rigidity, separation, conflict, inertia . . .) and was not expressing the qualities of love, truth and wisdom.

We must keep in mind that even under such conditions that we may have chosen, an evolving consciousness has energies to counterbalance the pull. For us, it is *evolution* and *education* (the powers that lead out and free the powers within).

As mentioned, the Cosmic Christ is the educator for our solar system, and thus the Earth itself is bathed in "educational" energies designed to unfold the Christ consciousness (a link to the Cosmic Christ) and potential within all lives using the Earth as its school.

The process was for the Christ to "stand" outside of the environment and to call the evolving lives to arise, carrying with them the treasures of experience and learning. We must keep in mind that evolvement on the Earth decrees involvement with the forces of materialization. The materialistic energies cannot assist consciousness to assimilate these experiences and turn them into wisdom. Only spiritual energies can turn experiences into understanding and wisdom.

The Cosmic Christ could not interfere directly nor deprive the evolving souls of their opportunity to grow through learning; to provide within themselves a counterbalance. Because of this though, greater beings came to the Earth to assist us as teachers and enlighteners (out of which developed the Qabala), but they were also limited since they were not part of the stream of consciousness of evolving life upon the Earth.

Because of this, and because of the scope of New Age energies that the Earth was moving toward, it was necessary for preparation of an individual so that he or she could link with the Cosmic Christ and begin to radiate the energies more directly within the earth plane itself. The more enlightened and more highly evolved of mankind began to put their efforts toward this objective. This was the start of the ancient Mystery Schools, and a more widely developed utilization of the Qabala to awaken spiritual energies that could turn the material experience into a force of wisdom.

Buddha was the first to be fully awakened to these energies and was able to form a direct link with the Christ, contacting and aligning his energies with the Cosmic Christ. Through the consciousness of Buddha, a bridge was formed between the Christ and all evolving life forms on Earth. Over the centuries this link strengthened. The energies flowed stronger and more fully onto the earth plane. It bridged the gulf which was necessary since most of mankind was unable to rise up and cross over. Through the Buddha, the Christ could begin to cross over to join mankind more directly.

The crossing over was completed through the energies of the Sixth Ray or Piscean Age which is drawing to a close. Through the energies of the Sixth Ray in conjunction with the Piscean energies affecting the Earth during its sojourn through the solar system, a foundation of love, devotion and idealism manifested and grounded itself upon the Earth.

Through the Master we call Jesus, the bridge and linkup and the crossing over of the Christ onto the Earth was completed. Through the consciousness of Jesus, the Cosmic Christ impregnated the aspects of higher love, devotion and idealism into the physical, etheric and spiritual bodies and life of the Earth, so that with each incarnation thereafter, these aspects would become more strongly ingrained and apparent within us. In this manner, the Cosmic Christ was able to relate to mankind directly.

Because it involved the consciousness of the one

we call Jesus, we need to be aware of its significance in relation to our topic, i.e. the Qabala, especially the Hebraic version. Jesus' early training was overseen by a sect of the Hebrew faith known as the Essenes. They were well versed in many of the so-called "occult" and mystical arts. They were trained in astrology, healing, herbology and the Qabala. Because of this training, especially in the Qabala, there is a stronger resonance within us toward the Hebraic form. It was also ingrained within our own physical, etheric and spiritual patterns as well. It reflects the energies most strongly affecting us as we prepare for the New Age.

To understand this even more, we need to examine the "Crucifixion." Through the Crucifixion (the "giving up of the Ghost"), the Cosmic Christ was placed within the cross of matter, time and space. The Cosmic Christ incarnated (with all its inherent energies) into the Earth itself and its very energy fabric *becoming a more intricate and apparent aspect of every soul and life upon the planet.* The energy of the Christ was implanted into the Earth and every soul, not to be released until the evolution of the lives of the Earth could attune to Him which now resided within each of us and thus release this *life back to its cosmic homeland. The Cosmic Christ no longer stood outside the evolution of Earth. He had entered the evolution itself and could now influence it more directly.*

Through the past 20 centuries, the seeds of cosmic energy and life, implanted within the womb of Mother Earth, have been germinating, gathering strength within the etheric fabric and level of all its beings. This preparation was vital, for without it we would not be able to handle or receive the outpourings of energy that come with the New Age.

Having been fully introduced and anchored within the Earth by the life and ministry of that soul Jesus, the Christ set about to accomplish the development of a new etheric pattern, powerful enough to offset the negative projections of human consciousness and pure enough to receive the outpourings of new energy from the Aquarian Age.

For this reason, use of the Hebraic system of the Qabala links us with the one who enabled this to take place: Jesus. It joins us more strongly with the system that opened up the Christ to Him and thus can facilitate the same within us. This is what is "hidden" in the Western Occult Tradition.

Further Exercises

1. Aside from the exercises already described, there are further variations that can provide some wonderful benefits and expansions of energy and consciousness. They help increase the understanding of the energies of the Qabala and further awaken us to their uses.

One of these is the building of the "Path of the Flaming Sword" within your consciousness. In this exercise, just as in the Middle Pillar, use the God Names in conjunction with visualizations of colors to awaken a higher realization. Starting with Kether, vibrate or intone the God Name for that sphere while visualizing a brilliant ball of crystalline light in the appropriate color for that sphere. In this case intone the name EHEIEH (Eh-Heh-Yeh) while visualizing a

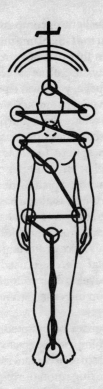

In this variation, again the God Names are repeatedly intoned as in a mantram, but in the order of actual manifestation from Kether to Malkuth. A period of meditation following the intonations of Malkuth will reveal much along many lines as to the various manifestations, both positive and negative, within your life. It is an excellent exercise to reveal greater insight into the effects of energy upon all levels of your being, not so much as separate and distinct levels but as interconnecting and interpenetrating levels of consciousness which can never be truly separated, one from the other.

ball of crystalline light encompassing the crown of your head. Repeat the God Name until you can actually feel the energy in that part of your being.

As you follow the path as depicted in the diagram on the previous page, you awaken each sephira in its turn. As you move from one sephira to the next, you should visualize a blue flame burning its way to the next level of consciousness. It is sometimes helpful to pause after each sphere to allow yourself time to digest and assimilate the experience.

By the time you finish with Malkuth, several things will occur. One is that you have turned yourself into a living sword of power. You have brought down into your physical, mundane life a very powerful, spiritual force. This force protects and shields, and the more this particular exercise is used, the more energy and control you develop over your life. It is an excellent exercise to develop increased strength and assertiveness.

This exercise can be adapted to accelerate the manifestation of things, ideas, creativity, new positions or even new levels of consciousness. It all depends on what you are focusing upon during the exercise. Because the Path of the Flaming Sword is symbolic of how all life manifested in this universe, it is an exercise that allows you to learn how to manifest things within your own "mini-universe," your life. Practice and meditation after the exercise will reveal how best you personally can utilize this exercise to alter your life conditions and to manifest higher fulfillment. Remember that the Tree of Life is a *living* tree and adapts itself to every individual in its own unique way.

These exercises are starting points, guidelines. They are not engraved in stone.

If we are to take greater responsibility for our own life, then we need to take what we can from whatever source we can, extract it, re-shape it and re-synthesize it into a system of perpetual growth that works for us as individuals.

2. Another method of coming in touch with all of the energies of the Tree of Life is to begin to build and stimulate the Tree of Life within the aura itself. The Tree of Life reflects all energies within the universe. Since we are a microcosm of the great macrocosm, then we also have within us all the energies. By learning to build the Tree of Life, to actually bring the Tree to life within our own energy fields, we stimulate and activate all the energies and potentials within us.

As in most of these exercises, the procedures are basically the same. As you become proficient, experiment and discover derivations that are more compatible and powerful for you. Begin with the sephira Kether and intone and visualize the God Name and color respectively for that sphere. By following the order of intonation as depicted in the following diagram, you build a tremendous circle of energy around you.

Notice from the diagram that in this exercise you do not follow the normal order. Energies awaken and flow within each one of us differently. You do not need to lock yourself into any specific order of activation as long as you can activate the energies and forces in a balanced manner. In this particular exercise start with Kether, and then move to Chokmah, Chesed,

Building the Tree of Life into the Aura

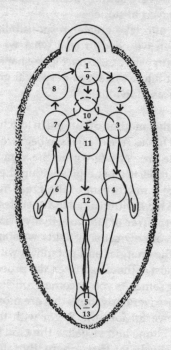

This diagram presents a technique for building the energy of the Tree of Life into the aura. One can use the God Names or Archangelic Names as both have very powerful effects. As the names for each sephira are intoned, repeatedly as in a mantram, the universal energy is set in motion and brought into rapport with the individual's energy. It awakens and balances all energies and all energy centers within the individual's essence. Since the last phase involves the sephiroth that constitute the Middle Pillar, tremendous balance is established. This exercise protects and seals the aura against negative or intrusive influences. It is good to do prior to contact with lots of people and at the end of the day to re-establish contact with your Higher Self.

Netzach, Malkuth, and then move upward to Hod, Geburah, Binah and back to Kether. This creates a powerful ring of energy that fortifies and seals the entire auric field. By intoning the God Names with each of these in this order, while visualizing the energy color for that sephira, you awaken and tap your highest energies for protection and stimulation.

As you return to Kether, repeat the vibrating of the God Name and continue with those sephiroth that constitute the Middle Pillar: Kether, Daath, Tiphareth, Yesod and Malkuth. This awakens a higher receptivity to all of the energies. With the ring formed by the outer sephiroth, bring the energies of your aura and your environment into harmony with your Higher Self. By concluding with the Middle Pillar, you complete the bridging of the outer consciousness with the inner. You link the inner and outer worlds, and you awaken to a greater understanding of the interplay of energies upon you at all times.

With these exercises it is always beneficial to conclude with a meditation to assist you in assimilating the experience and to receive higher guidance on your own personal adaptations. Because they are intensely energizing, after the meditations with each of these it is wise to conclude with the Qabalistic Cross to close your energy centers down and then to drink some water or eat something light to further ground the energies.

3. This next variation is one in which you can build an energy of angelic protection and guidance around you. If you recall, the spiritual experience that

comes from tapping and utilizing the energies and forces at that level of our consciousness that we refer to as Malkuth is "the Vision of the Holy Guardian Angel." This exercise is one that facilitates and accelerates you into touching that aspect of your being.

The procedure is the same as in building the entire Tree of Life within the aura. The difference lies in the using of the Archangelic Names instead of the God Names. Since there is more discernible contact and influence from Archangelic Name energies than those energies that resonate with the God Names themselves, this is an exercise that can create some dramatic effects.

Prior to performing this exercise, it might serve to list each of the Archangels of the sephiroth upon individual 3 x 5 index cards, and then to look up as much information about these beings. There are many sources that can describe these wondrous beings of Light; not only in their usual appearance, but the energy with which they come, the kinds of services and aid they can provide and even the usual colors associated with them. This assists and facilitiates the visualization and the calling forth to them through the intonation of their names.

As in the previous exercise, start with Kether. Visualize the Archangel Metatron, and using the information on the index cards, visualize him and his energy touching you as you slowly and repeatedly vibrate his name. Continue this focusing and vibrating until you can feel the change in the energy around you. It is noticeable, and even though it is not physical, it has a tangible feel to it. Everyone will experience it some-

Building a Tree of Angelic Protection and Guidance

what differently as this being's energy (as with them all) will interact uniquely with your own.

Continue this process for all of the sephiroth. Alter the order occasionally, and it will alter the experience. In the beginning, it is best to use the order as in the variation just described. By the time you finish, you *will* feel the brush of angel wings upon you. Meditate. Allow the communication to flow to you.

Remember that when you touch higher energies, it changes your own, increasing your own vibration. By the end of this exercise, you may feel as if you are surrounded by wings of ethereal energy. There is no experience quite like it. It is what makes working with the Qabala so wondrous. Everything we do with it expands our awareness and shows to us the rigid patterns that can block our growth. It opens to us perceptions and potential that can fill our lives with joy and light.

4. The last variation on the Middle Pillar exercise involves greater use of the force of colors within the Pillar. There exist many ways of focusing the energy around you and within you. This was discussesd to some degree in the earlier sections, and will be elaborated upon.

Color is an energy force. It is a concentration of energy at a certain vibrational level. This includes the universal energy that exists outside of you and around you at all times. It also includes the energy levels that exist within the various levels of your subconscious. By performing the Middle Pillar exercise, visualizing the colors for the sephiroth that become the Middle Pillar, you more specifically awaken and open the energies of that level in a balanced condition for you to utilize. Thus, rather than visualizing a brilliant, crystalline white light, building that pillar of balance within you, visualize the color of each sephira, linked by a flow of crystalline energy. (Refer to the diagram on the following page.)

For the sphere of Kether, continue to visualize the blinding white, crystalline light. Hidden within the color white are all colors. This has great significance, since it is from Kether that all other levels were created. Some sources suggest visualizing golden flecks within the white. Again, it is individual. Find and use what works best for you. It is this energy that opens the crown chakra and allows for a greater flow of energy into all other levels of your being. As it flows through you and awakens within you, it adds strength and vitality to all other levels of your consciousness. It is that level of your consciousness which is awakened so that you can more fully express your energies and abilities on all levels. It serves as your link to that ever abundant source of divine energy within the universe. It serves as the channel to flow to you and within you, to be utilized by your other levels of consciousness. It is the root of your spiritual essence that flows down to you within the physical. It is your link to the Divine, so that everything that flows from it has within it that Divinity. Visualizing the white and seeing the "floodgates" of spiritual energy being opened to flow into the other levels of consciousness is very important and beneficial.

Next visualize the crystalline energy flowing down into that level that was referred to earlier as Daath.

Colors of Energy in the Middle Pillar

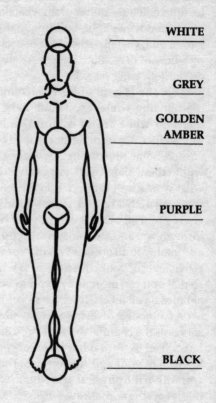

WHITE

GREY

GOLDEN
AMBER

PURPLE

BLACK

This diagram represents a technique for utilizing the colors as an energy stimulant in the Middle Pillar exercise. The colors associated with the sephiroth of the Middle Pillar are visualized during the intoning of the God Names (as in the other variations). Linking each of the spheres of the Middle Pillar, connecting each of the colors is the visualization of a channel of brilliant, crystalline energy.

Daath is a mysterious level within your consciousness whose significance will only be touched upon in this volume. It is associated with the throat chakra, the thyroid and that point where the spine meets the skull. It is at this level that the energy flowing to you in the Middle Pillar exercise is first transmuted so that you can more easily access it within your life. It serves as the bridge, so to speak, between the true spiritual essence and energy of your being, and that which becomes channeled and changed for use in your development and unfoldment through the various levels of your consciousness. All of the levels of consciousness below Daath on the Tree of Life are much more accessible because of the work of this level.

The color to visualize in this sphere is a grey or blue/grey, flecked with gold. Grey is the color of initiation. Behind the clouds of grey is the white light of spirituality. Activating this center through visualizing this color allows it to more fully draw greater energy from Kether to be utilized by all of the other levels of consciousness. It triggers the alchemical change, releasing and freeing greater energy to work with.

As the other levels of consciousness are activated, this level is stimulated and works with them to allow for greater knowledge to be released in those other levels of consciousness. It serves to "ground" the spiritual energy of your true essence so that it can be tapped through the other various levels of consciousness.

As the energy flows out of Daath into that center called Tiphareth, the vibration changes. Visualizing a golden amber sphere of scintillating light in the area of the heart will activate this center. The yellow releases the healing warmth of your own inner "sun" into your life. It stimulates creative energy and activity. It stimulates the heart chakra, which is the balancing energy center connected to the physical body. It mediates all of the others.

Visualizing this color releases energy into your aura of geniality, wholeness, well-being. It stimulates illumination. It helps to release higher forms of psychic and healing energy to you.

As the energy flows out of Tiphareth, it flows down into that level known as Yesod. As the energy flows into this level, it stimulates a release of energy to be utilized by you. Visualizing the color purple in this area facilitates this process.

The purple or violet color stimulates an activation of psychic consciousness, but it does so in a subtle manner. It awakens energy to be utilized for the use of magic. It adds strength to the Magical Body you are establishing, doing so in a balanced manner. It helps you to step back into the flow of your life, to recognize that there is a natural rhythm to the unfolding of events in your life. It enables you to more fully work and live within those rhythms, so that you can take advantage of the high points and balance out the low. The color awakens the energy so that you can gain control and direct your emotions in a manner that enables you to manifest that which you need or want more quickly and more strongly. It enables you to still the emotions so that conflict and struggle lessen in your life so that you can make further progress.

As the energy moves down to that level of your

being and consciousness closest to the normal waking state of consciousness, it changes again. It takes on another vibration and this is reflected through another color. The color predominant to visualize is black, or black with yellow flecks.

Black is the opposite of white. Malkuth in one sense is the opposite of Kether. And yet there are similarities. Just as with white, all of the color spectrum exists within blackness. It conceals the light. It is through Malkuth that the search begins for the light hidden within us.

The black also serves to ground the spiritual energy stimulated in Kether so that it can be focused and utilized within your physical life.

As you intone the God Name and visualize the color for each sephira within the Middle Pillar, you activate the release of these energies into your life. It can then serve you and work for you throughout the day. It serves to help you maintain balance while remaining strong within your daily activities.

Working with the Middle Pillar exercises or with any of the techniques described earlier is important. Daily practice is essential if you intend to awaken and take greater responsibility for your potentials. There will always be some who will protest that they do not have time to apply to these activities. First, with practice the process becomes easier and quicker, and an exercise that took thirty to forty minutes in the beginning can be mastered with practice to where it only takes ten minutes. Second, by working with these exercises, you release greater energy to yourself so that tasks and situations in your daily life are neither as draining nor as time consuming. You find you can handle them much easier and quicker.

With anything you are trying to learn, it is the initial efforts that are the most time consuming but are also the most critical. Setting aside some time during the day *for yourself* is essential. Yes, we all have other obligations, but our greatest obligation is to our own unfoldment, and if only for our own sanity and well-being, we need to designate some time during the day for ourselves.

For those with hectic schedules, the Middle Pillar exercise is essential. Using it as a daily exercise plants the seeds for creating a magical life. The first thing in the morning will serve to balance your energies, release greater amounts to be utilized during your work day. It opens up those levels of energy within you that you can then draw upon throughout the day. The work day then becomes less difficult, less draining and more fulfilling.

Utilizing it again as the last activity of the day before you go to sleep is also effective. It restores the balance that can be lost through contact with so many different individuals and their very different energies. It cleanses your energy so that the entire sleep time is not spent upon that process and it, more importantly, opens levels of your subconscious so that it can work for you as you explore other realms and dimensions in that "secret" night life called dreams. It keeps the energy building around you so that while awake and while asleep our Magical Body grows and strengthens and resonates more and more with your physical body and its consciousness.

Learning to utilize both the waking state and the "sleep" state is essential to learning to live a magical life. Even if you fall asleep while doing the Middle Pillar at night, you have set it in motion so that the Magical Body of your higher consciousness will continue the process for you.

If you change your imaginings, you change your world. This is what you are doing by working with the Qabala and all of its levels. Even though you may work with them initially as separate and distinct forces, each exercise shows you that there is only *one power*, regardless of how it manifests. And it will show you that there is only one you, *the magical you*, regardless of how you have been manifesting yourself.

That power that revolves the planets around our Sun and moves our Sun throughout the universe is the same power that circulates the blood and energy throughout our own bodies. And that power is *perfect fulfillment, perfect abundance, perfect prosperity and perfect love*. Each and every one of us, without exception, has the right to claim and manifest our own *perfect fulfillment, abundance, prosperity and love*. It is the exercises with the Qabala that provide the guidelines to this magical realization.

Chapter 8

Pathworking

Nature unaided fails.
                          —Occult aphorism

One cannot begin a study of the Qabala without learning of the process of self-initiation called "pathworking." Pathworking is a form of guided meditation, but it is much more. The meditation contains specific elements that trigger archetypal responses; not only within us as individuals but within the environment. The pathworking sets in motion a force that manifests in situations and experiences in our day-to-day life that force us to respond and grow. We, through the force of the meditation, encounter similar situations within our physical life so that we can more fully and more quickly learn the lesson associated with the path.

In the beginning of this book, we discussed the 32 Paths of Wisdom, another name for the Qabalistic technique of evolvement. These 32 paths included the ten spheres of consciousness and various passages that linked them together. At some point in our growth we need to take the awareness that we achieve through touching our various levels and utilize it more actively and more efficiently in our day-to-day life. We draw from the realms of our subconscious to apply to our conscious-level existences. We create in our lives experiences that test our awareness and knowledge. We do so in order to more fully comprehend it and open ourselves to even greater practical application. Without the application, the knowledge can never become wisdom and can never fully be utilized to our higher and greater benefit.

This is the purpose of pathworking. The pathworkings set in motion on all levels of our existence (especially the physical) events that will test us. This testing of our awareness, our goals, our hopes and desires is what entails the process of self-initiation. This is not a book that deals with the actual pathworkings. There is ample material to be found elsewhere on them, but it is important for the beginner to know about the process and what it can involve. It is important if only for the reason that the beginner does not become involved in something that he or she may not be capable of handling at the early stage of enfoldment. By presenting this information on the process and what can occur as a result, the author hopes to give the beginning student greater perspective in deciding when and how to proceed to that very important and powerful process known as pathworking.

There are 22 paths that actually link the spheres and can be termed true paths. These paths entail combining the energies found at the levels of consciousness and bringing them to bear more strongly upon the physical existence. These paths are doorways or keys for skrying in the spirit—spirit travel. They traverse the mind, the various bodies and the various planes of existence. They link the levels of our consciousness, activating the levels that they join in manners that astound and confound. By traveling them, one is able to more fully open up and awaken the resources in the various levels; it forces us to utilize what we are touching. It is the actual utilization that instills the higher wisdom.

Although the pathworking may seem just like any other guided meditation or mind fantasy, it is dangerous to allow such thoughts to occur. Pathworkings contain powerful symbols that force an awakening of our subconscious. Although the situations, experiences and workings are symbolic, they will also strongly affect the physical world. We must remember that whatever we do on other planes will seep down and create a similar situation on the physical or mundane level of existence. Those who doubt that their thoughts can create physical effects or that such a relationship exists between the planes of existence or who may have only intellectualized about it up to this point will come face to face with the reality of it. *All* planes of existence interpenetrate and we *will* experience this through the pathworkings.

If we are not ready to instigate those strong effects and changes in our lives, if we are not ready to create situations that will create stress and force growth and major decisions, if we have difficulty already handling the events of our lives then we had better not start *any* pathworking! The Qabala is a system of evolvement, and through the pathworkings, we instigate and activate experiences and situations in our lives that hasten our progress. We create dynamic experiences that will either force growth or create even greater confusion and turmoil because of our inability to handle the growth. The Qabala is a system of initiation and evolvement. It makes us face what we have refused to face, to search out our hidden fears, and either succumb to them or overcome them, thus opening ourselves to the higher knowledge and experience. Through the pathworkings we become the catalysts of our own lives, for by working the paths we place ourselves in a position of stripping away the "dross" of our mundane lives to reveal the light within. It is a process that can be as painful as it can be joyful. It brings upon us those situations, activates those stresses that must be dealt with in order for greater change to occur.

It is for this reason that great precaution should be used by the beginning student. It is true that we only experience and awaken those energies and situations of which we are capable. It is proportionate to our experience and wisdom, but that in itself can be overwhelming to the beginner. Serious thought must be given to pathworking for the beginning student. Often in our lives we think we can handle more than we are capable of, and it is easy to become overwhelmed and begin to drown in the experiences of our lives. We live in a society that creates a lot of stress. Are we capable of creating more and handling it even if it does lead to greater growth?

A little knowledge can be a dangerous thing. We can easily fool ourselves into thinking we are ready to take major steps in our growth. Remember that *discrimination* is the virtue of Malkuth, the physical world. Only we can decide when we are ready. By taking things slowly and easily, allowing our consciousness to unfold in a time and manner that suits it, we will know when we can begin to accelerate the process to an even greater degree. We can achieve much simply by increasing our awareness of the various levels of our consciousness and utilizing them to enhance our lives. As we begin to grow through that process and acquire greater control over the circumstances of our lives, then we can accelerate even more. Then is the time to initiate pathworking.

The Qabala acts as a conscious agent for transformation between the upper and lower worlds—the upper and lower levels of our consciousness. The raising of matter, energy and awareness from an ordinary level to a higher state and then bringing down and transmitting that energy and awareness from the higher to the more mundane is part of the work of the Qabalist. We can do it in a controlled manner, a manner that entails balance on all levels of our beings.

It must be stressed that if we undertake pathworking without a good foundation of how the energy and forces within the system of the Qabala operate, problems can occur. Contact with good and evil is to be expected. Power will be given to see how it will be handled and temptation in many forms will be encountered—with *all* the karmic ramifications of both. Your values will be challenged inwardly and in external situations as well. By doing the pathwork, we *invite the tests upon us.*

There are benefits to be achieved through the use of pathworkings. Enjoyment is the first. They do give the conscious, rational mind an opportunity to relax. They stretch and improve the imagination. They increase and improve the ability to visualize. They enhance concentration and they awaken hidden skills, ideas and inspirations. They do invoke and manifest initiations into higher realms, and they intensify the communication between the various levels of consciousness within our being to the benefit of our abilities. Pathworking will engage deeper levels of the mind which sometimes need to be coaxed out because the conscious mind has difficulty dealing with them. *We come face to face with ourselves on all levels.*

If we decide to accelerate our growth even further through the use of pathworking, there are dangers and precautions with which we should be familiar. The subjective world may grow too real for those who have difficulty coping with the real world. It can be addictive to those who have not developed the discipline of a controlled will and it can lead to withdrawal from the real world. A pathworking is a form of powerful ritual, and it is very easy to underestimate its ability to affect the physical world. It is easy to become "fairy charmed" and disappear into the world of the mind, leaving no trace of the person who used to be. It is there to explore and learn from and grow from, but not to escape reality. And some may not like having to face themselves for the path *will* reveal any weaknesses. That is part of the growth process.

These special meditations that are termed path-workings are powerful. Because of this, the student who undertakes them should have a basic understanding of the Qabala and how it works. To jump in (wanting to initiate yourself immediately), to move faster than you are capable of assimilating, will create trouble. We can use the Qabala to enhance our lives and create greater awareness, abundance and fulfillment in a controlled manner. It begins simply by learning to tap the various levels of our being. There is so much fruit to be gathered from that process alone that the idea of manifesting greater tests in our lives may become unnecessary and unwanted. Each individual will have to decide for themselves. How quickly or slowly you move and grow and awaken your potentials is up to you and you alone. Outlined in this book are methods that will provide great rewards in all levels of your life. All of the tools are there for you to use, but you must use them if they are to create a harvest of abundance and joy in your life.

Just as money can be a catalyst in the lives of every person it touches, the Qabala can be also. We have the capability of being supreme alchemists—creating change and wonder and magic in our lives, and we can do so in a manner that allows us to grow and adapt to our greater abilities and energies—until such time as we are ready to begin the paths to even greater self-initiation. Patience, discipline and discrimination must always be the watchwords.

What we must remember is that with pathworking the universal laws of manifestation are triggered. Very simply, to manifest anything—be it a quality, an ability or something material within our lives—is very simple if you know the laws upon which manifestation are based. It comes back to an aspect of *energy* that was discussed in an earlier chapter. Everything is energy in one form or another, and by learning to focus and concentrate that energy we can alter and transmute it into any form we may need or desire. Yes, there is a responsibility with such acts, but there is also opportunity to become the masters of our own destiny in the process. Pathworking in the Qabala is one of the more dynamic methods available to use and understand these laws of manifestation, especially in connection to our own individual spiritual growth.

The laws of manifestation operate for all—regardless of our awareness of them. They are impersonal and neutral. They are for everyone. Unfortunately, very few know how they operate or ever even recognize them within their lives.

Manifestation is not making something out of nothing. It is neither truly magical nor wondrously miraculous. It is not highly esoteric or workable by only the gifted or the initiated. It is simply a change of form or state or the condition of being. It deals with more than just money and things. One can manifest ideas, creativity, states of health and higher levels of consciousness as well. Manifestation is the translating or transmuting of energy from one level to another, whether it is a level of our life or a level of our consciousness. It is that process which releases our potentials. It is not just a bringing down. It is an elevating. This, more than anything else, is what true pathworking should demonstrate.

The implications of considering manifestation in this manner are astounding. It implies that whatever we are wishing to manifest already exists for us somewhere within the universe. It also implies that if we know how, we can manifest anything we need or want in our life. These principles of manifestation operate according to natural law—the laws that govern life in the physical.

The first is the law of cause and effect. This means that "As you sow, so shall you reap." It requires that if you plant wheat seeds, then wheat and not corn will grow from them. These natural laws which we must abide require a time phase while in the physical. In other words, seeds that are planted require time to germinate, take root and then sprout. It is not instantaneous; something does *not* come from nothing. This is why we who work with the Qabala practice such techniques as pathworking. It provides a means of overriding to some degree the time phase and allows us to manifest conditions and energies at an accelerated pace. For the true seeker upon the path to higher enlightenment, it provides a method for taking on karma at a rapid rate. It provides accelerated lessons in life and consciousness. It is also the process of *remaining creative enough to produce good karma and to endure the suffering and trials of accelerated growth, while at the same time being efficient enough to continue doing good for mankind.* This is that phase of higher evolvement known as "discipleship."

In order to comprehend just how it operates in our own lives, we must look upon it as putting forth energy on all levels of our being: mental, emotional, physical, as well as spiritual. Only by learning to focus our energies on all of these levels simultaneously can we develop control over the circumstances of our lives.

At the heart of the Tree of Life is that level of consciousness known as Tiphareth. If you recall, the God-Force operating at that level is Jehovah Aloah va-Daath or "God made manifest in the Sphere of the Mind." This implies that at the heart of all life upon the physical and at the heart of all manifestations and transmutations of energy is the mind itself. This is true! Manifestation begins on the mental level. Thought is a tremendous force within the universe. It is our most effective force while in physical incarnation. Thought molds universal energy to begin the process of manifestation. We must remember that energy can be focused into an active force in many ways. Thought is one such way.

As discussed earlier, there is within our subconscious a level that operates the focusing of thought to instigate the concentration of universal energy to manifest things and conditions in our lives. This level operates in a very literal manner. If we think about how we catch two colds every winter, then that part of our subconscious begins its work to manifest the conditions that allow us to catch two colds every winter. Our thoughts become self-fulfilling prophecies. Thus we need to learn to control our thought processes, to cancel anything negative or detrimental and replace it with the positive. This involves increased attention to our thinking and increased concentration and visualization. This does require the use of will power, but we must remember that will power is not the same as force.

The guided meditations (called pathworkings) start the visualization that triggers the focusing of mental energy upon the various purposes. But this mental visualization is not enough. *Emotional energy* needs to be added to this. It is for this reason that most techniques for the pathworkings involve adventures that stimulate emotional responses in the individual. It is this emotional stimulation of the meditation that gives the actual mental visualization its push, further focusing the energy, drawing it down from the mental plane of existence upon which we operate as fully as on the physical and then enjoining it with the energy of the astral or emotional plane of existence. This astral plane is that plane of life energy closest to physical life.

The astral plane is a very fluid, changeable plane of existence. Because of this, the element of water is often a symbol for astral energies. It is in a state of continual change, affected constantly by every change of thought or feeling. It is composed of elemental essences from which shapes emerge continually and into which they also disappear. There are hundreds of varieties of energy manifestations in every level of the astral plane.

There are many currents of energy and light upon the astral which tend to carry a person every which way if they are not in control or do not have some strength of will. It is fluid and emotional and can create the same effect within us if care is not taken. It is for this reason that caution is advised for the beginning pathworker. Most of the experiences in the beginning are astral experiences, and regardless of what is seen or experienced, knowledge upon the astral does not necessarily reflect knowledge upon the physical or knowledge upon the spiritual. This is why the lesson of Malkuth is so emphasized. *Discriminate in all things!* It is absolutely important upon the path of higher evolvement.

Unreliability of impression occurs frequently upon the astral without proper training and patience. This is because the inhabitants are changeable, and also because sight in the astral plane is different from the physical sight. It is because of this that the method described earlier provides a safeguard and a means of opening access to the astral worlds, but in a controlled and safeguarded manner. Using the magical images, in conjunction with the Names of Power, the God and Archangelic Names, opens up the astral plane in a manner that permits exploration and higher realization, but with safety and control. These names and images have the power upon this plane. They protect while at the same time permitting entrance and exploration. By following this manner, when it comes time to work with pathwork itself, the student has been initiated into the astral plane, has done so in a protected manner and is thus more capable of utilizing the manifestation capabilities of a pathworking to its fullest extent. By following the technique described earlier, one develops balance and discrimination which are very essential for the actual pathworking process. We then manifest the powers of the paths.

This book was written in order to lay the foundation that permits greater utilization and awakening of our potentials at a highly accelerated rate. The methods to build upon this volume—including a detailed examination of the process of pathworking—will be described in the next volume. We cannot run before we walk, but through this volume, the course is mapped out, the stretching and warming up of spiritual muscles can take place and these techniques can be utilized to expand our awareness and perceptions in order to more fully take advantage of those gifts and techniques which can open us to worlds not yet even imagined.

Using the methods described in the earlier chapters will enable you to more fully prepare your consciousness to that accelerated process of growth known as pathworking. For the beginner, this is most essential, particularly when he/she makes contact with the astral plane of existence. These are many astral and enhanced psychic abilities that can be developed and used by anyone following these techniques. It is there for all. The astral plane interpenetrates physical life for everyone. Learning to utilize this plane of existence in order to enhance our own spiritual growth is a major first step, but it is also a step that can trip us up.

There are many miscellaneous astral phenomena that can be experienced and developed and manifested as part of our development through the Qabala. These include such things as clairvoyance, clairsentience, psychic healing, spirit communication, apports, materialization, levitation, slate writing, fire handling, transmutation of metals, the production of fire, and

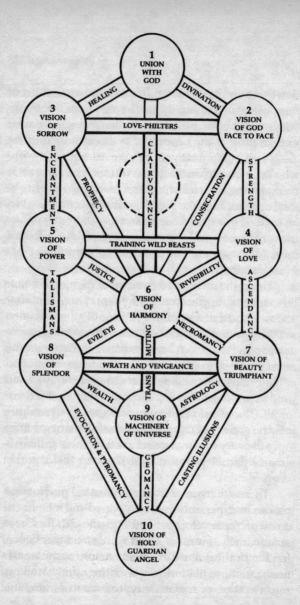

Magical Powers

many others. There are those though who will state that such abiliites can also be developed through mediumship. We must keep in mind that mediumship is *not* a power, it is a *condition*. With mediumship, the individual assumes a more passive role. With the Qabala, we are working to develop actively while maintaining control. Genuine mediumship can be utilized to enhance Qabalistic studies and development, but it requires control.

Almost all astral phenomena involve an increased sensitivity to the vibrations and energies of the astral plane. With the Qabala we learn to direct them and handle them and even to go beyond them, rather than just developing receptivity to them. There are often those who declare, "I have my contacts, my visions, and I know that all knowledge and power is within my own heart. What more can be added?" The answer is that knowledge of the techniques and psychology of higher consciousness available through the Qabala will enable them to keep the visions unimpaired and protect them from the many dangers of which they may be unaware. The untrained sensitive or medium can fall easily into using and abusing their abilities— often without true realization. Remember that higher development strongly affects the mind.

Increased sensitivity can render the psychic suspicious and quarrelsome. Any force which he or she does not understand is "evil." Those with increased sensitivity are aware of it and will defend themselves from undue influence by a ready suspiciousness and a fiery resentment. Touching with the astral plane can result in this hypersensitivity. This kind of individual is receptive and negative (in the sense of control) upon the astral, and thus is swept backwards and forwards by every astral wind that blows. This manifests in many neurotic conditions and actions in the physical; he/she may be blamed for his treachery, malice and changeability, but as a matter of fact, he/she is a victim much in the manner a child acquires a cold or measles. The germs were about, and the individual did not take precautions or did not know how.

Utilizing the techniques in this volume and those which will be presented in Volume II on the pathworking techniques will enable you to develop and open up your abilities in a controlled, disciplined and safe manner. We learn to step and then walk and then run—each with its advantages. In this manner, we then are able to discriminate and actively take charge of what we manifest in our lives whether it is a new state of consciousness or a new job. The process is the same, but as with any new skill we should not look for shortcuts, but develop our skills with care and caution. We take upon ourselves the responsibility for our lives and for all that occurs within them. We write the scripts. And it is the Qabala which shows us how we can change the plot, the actions, the characters, and most importantly the outcome.

Chapter 9

Creation

Go and catch a falling star,
*   Get with child a mandrake root,*
Tell me where all past years are,
*   Or who cleft the devil's foot,*
Teach me to hear mermaids singing,
Or to keep off envy's stinging,
*   And find*
*   What wind*
Serves to advance an honest mind.

                                    —John Donne

We are living in an exciting and powerful time. We are at the cusp between two great Ages, the Piscean and the Aquarian. On the deepest level of our consciousness we are all undergoing a spiritual transformation. We are being challenged to let go of the old and create the new, to leave the old life that we may find a new. We are all experiencing in our own ways and through our own unique situations aspects of the universal lesson of life and death. They go together. There cannot be one without the other.

Because of this we are all experiencing many changes. For many, the changes are distressing. The world situation and our personal lives may seem to go from bad to worse. Much that worked before no longer does. The fact is that many things *are* falling apart and will continue to do so with even greater intensity. But that is not negative! It is only upsetting to the degree that we remain emotionally attached to the old way of life or to the degree that we focus on the old rather than upon the infinite possibilities within the new.

No matter how great or small, changes and transformations are blessings. They are signals that there is growth. They are signs that we can achieve fulfillment, but only if we have room for it within our lives. Changes don't come from without, they come from within. The world is our mirror. As we change, everything reflected in it changes. And if we are to achieve the blessings that come from changes, we must take responsibility for our lives. This means opening ourselves to the innate power within us, and it is this which allows us to create the circumstances of our lives.

The Qabala prevents us from shortsightedness in our lives. It is very easy to become wrapped up in the situations within our own little worlds. The Qabala opens up the world, it lets the light shine into it. We cannot view our lives and our situations with blinders. The Qabala shows us the intricacies, the interrelatedness, the energies and forces that are available to each and every one of us. And it only requires touching upon them to a minute extent to alter our entire world.

The Qabala teaches us respect and reverence for all the manifestations of the Divine within the universe: past, present, seen and unseen. It demonstrates to us that we are not confined to the present. It teaches us how to alter our past and create our future. Man is a wanderer. He makes many pilgrimages within his lifetime. We each have our own little quests whether we conceive of them materially or metaphysically. To some degree there is always something over the next hill for each of us.

We are pilgrims upon the path of evolvement and regardless of whether or not we know the vast depths of time and space which we must tread, it should not destroy the adventure of the journey. There is *no* law, natural, spiritual or cosmic, that requires man to suffer and struggle without life or joy through his experiences. It is our concentrated focus upon our situations, their difficulties and the destination they are taking us to that binds us. It is also what blinds us to the adventures and discoveries that we could encounter along the way. It is what robs us of the wonder and delight of our earthly trek.

The Qabala shows us how to reestablish balance within our lives by awakening us to the energies within us that give us control over our growth, our circumstances and our being. For those just starting their journeys, go with joy and wonder and excitement. It is by traveling with our focus upon these that will allow us to experience them in their fullest.

When we withdraw our senses from our physical world, we enter an entirely different realm of existence. It is one which acts upon the physical, but operates according to different laws. It is one which we can tap and utilize to our greater benefit in the physical. The Qabala shows us how in a manner that provides balance. Too often we have allowed ourselves only to view things in one manner, and as we move away from that limited perspective, we find ourselves in a position to acquire nourishment and life from sources of which we had never dreamt.

It is through learning to tap the resources of these inner realms that we learn to utilize our energies and potentials to impact upon our lives and our environments. We have the capability of working with energy at all levels. We can bind it, transfer it, break it down, build it up and transmute it. We are surrounded and permeated by tremendously awesome powers—powers that might seem to diminish us, and yet we have great control. We are not at their mercy. We have the power to create and destroy, to act or not to act. We have the power to use or not to use. We, in essence, have the power to choose. We have the power of life and death. Life is choosing to use the divine energy within. Death is choosing to block or go against the energy that is ours to utilize by right. The choice is always ours, and each time we trust and utilize it to impact upon our lives with love and joy, our divine channels open up further and more life flows within our being. Virtually, our cells revive, become renewed and revitalized, and physically, mentally and emotionally we become stronger. And the divine energy that is our essence shines through.

The important thing about utilizing our energies is to do so in as clear manner as possible. We need to strip away the "metaphysical jargon" and cut to the meat of the matter. We must use our awareness to deal with our life situations. If we don't, we do little more than dabble, and dabbling always brings its own difficulties. We don't need more.

Traditionally there are two types of people who are actively involved in the opening of themselves and their awareness. And this occurred even in the ancient Mystery School. The first were those who were interested in learning the techniques on how to use energy and manifest it through physical demonstrations—be it higher clairvoyance, healing or other such acts. They were more concerned with the principles to master certain types of activity but were not interested in the spiritual precepts that these activities were based upon and which could lead to an ideal state of being. It is the difference between the casual and insincere seeker and the one who was sincere.

Today, this can be seen quite often within the metaphysical and spiritual field as well. There are still those who run around, hopping from psychic reader to psychic reader, teacher to teacher, gathering books and ever seeking the truths of life. But they never truly understand the workings of the truths they have gathered. The understanding comes with us and with practice. It involves responsibility.

Magic is not a charm or spell or method to manifest some special person or thing within your life. Magic is not a retreat from life. It is not an escape from the situations we encounter. Magic is an initiation into a higher understanding of our own responsibility for the course and circumstance of our existence. Magic is the utilization of this higher awareness to recreate our life upon a higher realm.

There are many teachers, many ideologies, many philosophies and religious denominations. We do not have to limit ourselves to one, we can gain something from them all. Being responsible means that we take what we can find from whatever source we can find, extract it, re-shape it and synthesize it into a system of *perpetual growth* that works for us individually. It is using what we learn in the manner that is best for us. It is recognizing that there is *no one* doing anything that we also cannot do *in our own unique manner!*

Above the portals of the ancient Mystery Schools was but one commandment: "Know thyself!" Within each of us is the capability of releasing that infinite potential to manifest greater enlightenment, fulfillment, love and light in all arenas of our life. The recognition of this and then the utilization of it is what makes all the wonder and magic of life.

The world is a world of *color* and *light* and *joy*. It is a world that we can fashion to our highest dreams and ideals. It is a world that *all* may enter with openness and reverence, for this is also God's world.

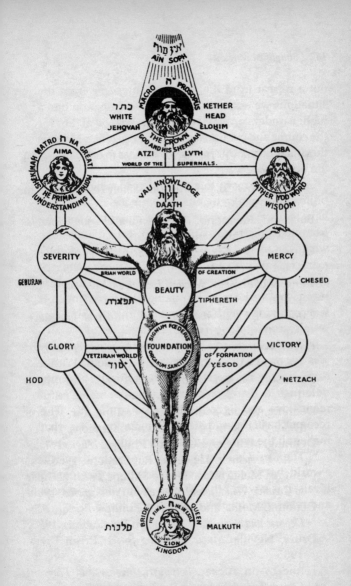

The Sacred Tree of the Sephiroth

(Published by arrangement with Lyle Stuart, Inc.)

Bibliography

Albertus, Frater. *The Seven Rays of the QBL.* Samuel Weiser.

Ashcroft-Nowicki, Dolores. *The Shining Paths.* Aquarian Press, 1983.

Buckland, Raymond. *Practical Candleburning Rituals.* Llewellyn Publications, 1982.

Cunningham, Scott. *Cunningham's Encyclopedia of Magical Herbs.* Llewellyn Publications, 1985.

Cunningham, Scott. *Magical Herbalism.* Llewellyn Publications, 1983.

Cooper, J. C. *Symbolism—The Universal Language.* Aquarian Press, 1982.

David, William. *The Harmonics of Sound, Color and Vibration.* DeVorss and Company, 1980.

Davidson, Gustaf. *Dictionary of Angels.* Free Press, 1967.

Denning, Melita and Osborne Phillips. *The Magical Philosophy, Books I-V.* Llewellyn Publications, 1978.

Denning, Melita and Osborne Phillips. *Magical States of Consciousness.* Llewellyn Publications, 1985.

Denning, Melita and Osborne Phillips. *Practical Guide to Creative Visualization.* Llewellyn Publications, 1980.

Denning, Melita and Osborne Phillips. *Psychic Self-Defense and Well-Being.* Llewellyn Publications, 1985.

Drury, Neville. *Music for Inner Space.* Prism Press, 1985.

Fettner, Ann Tucker. *Potpourri, Incense and Fragrant Concoctions.* Workman Publishing, 1977.

Fortune, Dion. *Applied Magic.* Aquarian Press, 1979.

Fortune, Dion. *Esoteric Orders and Their Work.* Aquarian Press, 1982.

Fortune, Dion. *The Mystical Qabala.* Ernst Benn Limited, 1979.

Fortune, Dion. *Practical Occultism in Daily Life.* Aquarian Press, 1981.

Frank, Adolphe. *The Kabbalah.* Bell Publishing, 1960.

Gawain, Shakti. *Creative Visualization.* Whatever Publishing, 1978.

Gray, William G. *Concepts of the Qabalah.* Samuel Weiser, 1984.

Gray, William G. *Magical Ritual Methods.* Samuel Weiser, 1980.

Halevi, Z'ev ben Shimon. *Adam and the Kabbalistic Tree.* Samuel Weiser, 1985.

Halevi, Z'ev ben Shimon. *The Work of the Kabbalist.* Samuel Weiser, 1984.

Hall, Manly P. *Magic.* Philosophical Research Society, 1978.

Heline, Corinne. *Music: The Keynote of Human Evolution.* New Age Bible and Philosophy Center.

Highfield, A. C. *Symbolic Weapons of Ritual Magic.* Aquarian Press, 1983.

Hodson, Geoffrey. *The Kingdom of the Gods.* Theosophical Publications, 1952.

Jung, Carl. *Archetypes and the Great Unconscious.*

Jung, Carl. *Collected Works (Vol. 18) —The Symbolic Life.* Princeton University Press, 1976.

Knight, Gareth. *Practical Guide to Qabalistic Symbolism.* Samuel Weiser, 1978.

Lewis, H. Spencer. *Mystical Life of Jesus.* Rosicrucian

Press, 1944.

Lewis, H. Spencer. *The Secret Doctrines of Jesus*. Rosicrucian Press, 1954.

Miller, Richard Alan. *Magical and Ritual Use of Herbs*. Destiny Books, 1983.

Price, Shirley. *Practical Aromatherapy*. Thorsons Publishing, 1983.

Regardie, Israel. *Complete Golden Dawn System of Magic*. Falcon, 1984.

Regardie, Israel. *Ceremonial Magic*. Aquarian Press, 1980.

Regardie, Israel. *A Garden of Pomegranates*. Second edition. Llewellyn Publications, 1985.

Regardie, Israel. *The Golden Dawn*. Llewellyn Publications, 1982.

Regardie, Israel. *The One Year Manual*. Samuel Weiser, 1981.

Regardie, Israel. *The Tree of Life*. Samuel Weiser, 1972.

Reed, Ellen Cannon. *The Witches' Qabala*. Llewellyn Publications, 1986.

Richardson, Alan. *Gate of Moon*. Aquarian Press, 1984.

Roche de Coppens, Peter. *The Nature and Use of Ritual*. Llewellyn Publications, 1985.

Schure, Edouard. *The Great Initiates*. Harper and Row, 1961.

Schure, Edouard. *From Sphinx to Christ*. Harper and Row, 1970.

Sturzaker, James. *Aromatics in Ritual and Therapeutics*. Metatron Publications, 1979.

Sturzaker, D. & J. *Colour and the Kabbalah*. Samuel Weiser, 1975.

Suares, Carlo. *The Qabala Trilogy*. Shambhala Publications, 1985.

Tame, David. *The Secret Power of Music.* Destiny Books, 1984.

Vinci, Leo. *Candle Magic.* Aquarian Press, 1981.

Vinci, Leo. *Incense.* Aquarian Press, 1980.

Waite, A. E. *The Holy Kabbalah.* University Books/ Citadel Press.

Wand, Robert. *The Qabalistic Tarot.* Samuel Weiser, 1983.

Weinstein, Marion. *Positive Magic.* Phoenix Publishing, 1978.

On the following pages you will find listed, with their current prices, some of the books now available on related subjects. Your book dealer stocks most of these and will stock new titles in the Llewellyn series as they become available. We urge your patronage.

TO GET A FREE CATALOG

To obtain our full catalog, you are invited to write (see address below) for our bi-monthly news magazine/catalog, *Llewellyn's New Worlds of Mind and Spirit*. A sample copy is free, and it will continue coming to you at no cost as long as you are an active mail customer. Or you may subscribe for just $10 in the United States and Canada ($20 overseas, first class mail). Many bookstores also have *New Worlds* available to their customers. Ask for it.

TO ORDER BOOKS AND TAPES

If your book store does not carry the titles described on the following pages, you may order them directly from Llewellyn by sending the full price in U.S. funds, plus postage and handling (see below).

Credit card orders: VISA, MasterCard, American Express are accepted. Call us toll-free within the United States and Canada at 1-800-THE-MOON.

Postage and Handling: Include $4 postage and handling for orders $15 and under; $5 for orders *over* $15. There are no postage and handling charges for orders over $100. Postage and handling rates are subject to change. We ship UPS whenever possible within the continental United States; delivery is guaranteed. Please provide your street address as UPS does not deliver to P.O. boxes. Orders shipped to Alaska, Hawaii, Canada, Mexico and Puerto Rico will be sent via first class mail. Allow 4-6 weeks for delivery. **International orders:** Airmail – add retail price of each book and $5 for each non-book item (audiotapes, etc.); Surface mail – add $1 per item.

Minnesota residents please add 7% sales tax.

Llewellyn Worldwide
P.O. Box 64383 L-015, St. Paul, MN 55164-0383, U.S.A.

For customer service, call (612) 291-1970.

MODERN MAGICK
by Donald Michael Kraig

Modern Magick is the most comprehensive step-by-step introduction to the art of ceremonial magic ever offered. The eleven lessons in this book will guide you from the easiest of rituals and the construction of your magickal tools through the highest forms of magick: designing your own rituals and doing pathworking. Along the way you will learn the secrets of the Kabbalah in a clear and easy-to-understand manner. You will discover the true secrets of invocation (channeling) and evocation, and the missing information that will finally make the ancient grimoires, such as the "Keys of Solomon," not only comprehensible, but usable. This book also contains one of the most in-depth chapters on sex magick ever written. *Modern Magick* is designed so anyone can use it, and it is the perfect guidebook for students and classes.

0-87542-324-8, 592 pgs., 6 x 9, illus., softcover $14.95

MAGICAL GATEWAYS
by Alan Richardson

Originally published as *An Introduction to the Mystical Qabalah* (1974, 1981), *Magical Gateways* is the revised and substantially expanded re-release of of this excellent introduction to the essentials of magic.

Explore the *theories and principles* behind ritual practice (i.e., the Middle Pillar and the Lesser Banishing Ritual) that other books only touch upon. Explore the Qabalah—the Tree of Life—as it applies to daily living, perform astral magic, use the Tarot for self-exploration, relate mythology to your own life to gain greater self-knowledge, revisit past lives, build patterns in your aura, banish unpleasant atmospheres and create gates into other dimensions.

This is the world of *real* magic, in which an understanding of the Qabalah forms the first step in a radical transformation of personal consciousness.

0-87542-681-6, 208 pgs., mass market, illus. $4.95

A KABBALAH FOR THE MODERN WORLD
Migene González-Wippler

A *Kabbalah for the Modern World* was the first book to present the Kabbalah from a scientific orientation and show how it clearly relates to such modern scientific models as Quantum Theory, Relativity and the Big Bang. Now this Kabbalah classic has been revised and expanded to include a larger bibliography and new section: The Kabbalah of Wisdom. This new section includes never before published information and rituals, making this fascinating book more important than ever!

This book is not merely a "magical manual." It is far more than that. It is a journey into new dimensions of being, self-discovery and spiritual development. Above all, it is a search for "devekkut," the true union with the Godhead. Reading *A Kabbalah for the Modern World* is a unique experience. You will grow inwardly as you read, as your spirit comprehends the message ... and you will never, ever be the same again.

0-87542-294-2, 304 pgs. 5 ¼ x 8, softcover $9.95

THE GOLDEN DAWN
The Original Account of the Teachings,
Rites & Ceremonies of the Hermetic Order
As revealed by Israel Regardie

Complete in one volume with revision, expansion, and additional notes by Regardie, Cris Monnastre, and others. Also included are Initiation Ceremonies, important rituals for consecration and invocation, methods of meditation and magical working based on the Enochian Tablets, studies in the Tarot, and the system of Qabalistic Correspondences that unite the World's religions and magical traditions into a comprehensive and practical whole. This volume is designed as a study and suited to both group and private practice. Ceremonies are fully experiential without need of participation in group or lodge. A complete reference encyclopedia of Western Magick.

0-87542-663-8, 840 pgs., 6 x 9, illus., softcover $24.95